The International Debt Crisis of the Third World

By the same author:

Ölpreisschocks und wirtschaftliche Entwicklung: Anpassungsprobleme in der Dritten Welt (with J.P. Agarwal and H.H. Glismann) J.C.B. Mohr.

The International Debt Crisis of the Third World:

Causes and Consequences for the World Economy

Peter Nunnenkamp

Research Fellow
The Kiel Institute of World Economics

DISTRIBUTED BY HARVESTER PRESS

First published in Great Britain in 1986 by
WHEATSHEAF BOOKS LTD
A MEMBER OF THE HARVESTER PRESS PUBLISHING GROUP
Publisher: John Spiers
Director of Publications: Edward Elgar
16 Ship Street, Brighton, Sussex

British Library Cataloguing in Publication Data
Nunnenkamp, Peter
    The International debt crisis of the Third
    World: causes and consequences for the
    world economy.
    1. Debts, External—Developing countries
    I. Title
    336.3'435'091724   HJ8899
    ISBN 0-7108-0752-X

Phototypeset in 11 point Times Roman by Tradespools Ltd, Frome
Printed and bound in Great Britain by
Biddles Ltd, Guildford and King's Lynn

THE HARVESTER PRESS PUBLISHING GROUP
The Harvester Press Publishing Group comprises Harvester Press
Limited (chiefly publishing literature, fiction, philosophy, psy-
chology, and science and trade books), Harvester Press Microform
Publications Limited (publishing in microform unpublished
archives, scarce printed sources, and indexes to these collections)
and Wheatsheaf Books Limited (a wholly independent company
chiefly publishing in economics, international politics, sociology
and related social sciences), whose books are distributed by The
Harvester Press Limited and its agencies throughout the world.

To Erbse and Tulpe

Contents

List of Tables

Preface

The affluent, industrialised North normally seems rather apathetic to the economic difficulties of the developing South. With enough of problems of their own, politicians, the press and the public in the North do not bother much about the problems of the South. No doubt pictures of the poor faced by starvation do evoke some human cordiality in the rich, but only to the extent of writing cheques in favour of some charitable institution to appease their troubled conscience. At the same time, the rich accuse the 'low-wage countries' of the South of dumping and thus, it is said, significantly adding to unemployment in the North. In joint action, employers and employees in industrialised countries lobby for protectionism and countervailing measures, and politicians comply with these requests, although it is obvious that an artificial protection of domestic industries in the North will further aggravate the misery of the South.

The scenario seemed to have changed in the early eighties with Brazil, Mexico and some other heavily indebted Third World countries declaring that they were unable to meet their foreign debt obligations. The Third World's economic difficulties became a major issue of public debate in industrialised countries. However, this was not because of a rising interest in developing countries' well-being *per se*. It was rather the widespread fear that the debt problems of some of the Third World's major borrowers could adversely affect the economic well-being of the industrialised countries which caused considerable concern. Developing countries' defaults, when added to the repayment difficulties already experienced by Eastern Bloc nations, it was argued, could severely impede the smooth functioning of world financial markets. Widespread failures of commercial banks which were heavily engaged in lending to the Third World could even result in a collapse of the international financial system. Frequently, the threat of another worldwide depression, comparable to the one half a century ago, was conjured up.

Since then the mood of panic has cooled somewhat. Politicians, banks and international organisations, in joint effort, have mounted quick rescue operations which have provided quite a few developing countries with additional funds. The crisis management has so far succeeded in preventing the Third World's repayment difficulties from substantially affecting the world economy. However, the underlying problems have been postponed rather than solved. Major repayment difficulties are expected to recur in the second half of the eighties, when huge debt repayments, recently postponed, will fall due.

Moreover, there is still a considerable degree of confusion regarding the Third World's debt situation:

1. Notwithstanding a significant improvement in the data base, information on the external indebtedness remains far from complete.
2. Many analyses of underlying factors are rather one-sided. Frequently, debt problems are exclusively attributed to 'anonymous' world market developments. The responsibility of both debtors and creditors remains inadequately exposed.
3. Possible worldwide repercussions arising from borrowers' repayment difficulties are still heavily disputed between rather pessimistic and more optimistic observers.
4. Considerable disagreement also prevails as to how to ease the developing countries' debt burden and how to prevent international ramifications.

This list already indicates the central topics of this book. Besides presenting a short global overview on the Third World's foreign indebtedness in Chapter 1, the first part of the book endeavours to identify important differences in the debt situation of different developing country groups (Ch. 2) and eighteen major individual borrowing countries (Ch. 3). This part culminates in an attempt to discriminate between sound borrowers and problem borrowers in Chapter 4. This analysis forms the basis for the following investigation.

The second part that focuses on the causes of the recent debt crises in the Third World comprises of three more chapters. The first (Ch. 5) questions the widely held view that difficulties in servicing foreign debt are the inevitable consequence of unforeseen external shocks which were outside the control of both debtors and creditors. This view is further challenged thereafter. Chapter 6 stresses the relevance of borrowing countries' economic policies in becoming a problem borrower or not. Chapter 7 analyses the lending attitudes of Western commercial banks, which nowadays are the most important creditors of the Third World's largest debtor nations. The question is posed whether the banks bear part of the responsibility for the borrowers' debt problems.

Turning to possible worldwide consequences of developing countries' defaults in the third part, Chapter 8 presents a comparison of economic conditions prevailing in the twenties and thirties on the one hand and in the early eighties on the other. In this way we may discover whether the Great Depression is really the relevant point on which to focus in view of the present economic tensions. Chapter 9 discusses in some more detail the probability of bank failures and possible chain reactions.

The question as to how to tackle the Third World's debt problems is dealt with in the subsequent chapters. The practice of rescheduling, and especially the role of the International Monetary Fund in it, is critically reviewed (Ch. 10). Since the success of short-term emergency programmes critically depends on an improvement in the international economic environment, Chapter 11 tries to assess whether there are reasonable prospects that debt-service obligations will become easier to handle in the near future. Even those who are rather optimistic about future developments in world markets will largely agree that debt problems cannot be solved exclusively by simply postponing the repayment of foreign loans. The short-term approach has to be supplemented. That is why the proposals which are intended to ease the developing countries' debt situation in the longer run are evaluated in Chapter 12. Finally, Chapter 13 summarises the main elements of a longer-term solution; specific reference is made to the question of defining the lender-of-last-resort function of monetary institutions.

I owe thanks especially to my colleagues in the Kiel Institute of World Economics, who gave me the chance to write this book and who contributed in various ways to its realisation. In particular, I wish to record by appreciation for the assistance provided by Kusum Ravinder Bhatia. She worked through hundreds of newspaper-cuttings in order to get a detailed impression of the different aspects of debt problems experienced by eighteen sample countries in the very recent past. This arduous task formed the basis of the summary table presented in Chapter 4. Furthermore, I am most grateful to her for reading the complete manuscript and for suggesting many improvements.

I have to apologise to Dean Spinanger for frequently disturbing him in his own work because, over and over again, I had to ask him for stylistic advice. Ulrich Lächler and Georg Junge were always prepared to discuss the different aspects of the Third World's international indebtedness. Many thanks also to them for constructive criticism after having read the manuscript.

Valuable assistance was also provided by Michaela Rank, who did most of the computational work and by Barbara Buss, who typed and retyped the whole of this book through successive drafts.

Part I
THE SETTING

1 Developing Countries' Deteriorating Debt Situation

Twice in the last decade the non-oil developing countries (NOPECs)[1] have experienced a sharp rise in their current-account deficits. Following the oil-price explosion in 1973/74, the net total of balances on goods, services and private transfers resulted in a deficit of $46 billion in 1975, more than four times that of 1973. The NOPECs had just succeeded in improving their current-account position to some extent when the second oil-price crisis of 1979/80 occurred. Combined with economic stagnation, intensified protectionist pressures in the industrialised world and the NOPECs' own domestic policy mistakes, this oil-price hike contributed to a renewed steep rise in deficits, which in 1981 exceeded $100 billion.

It was not only the large financial needs but also some obvious structural changes in their capital account that caused concern for the NOPECs' balance of payments situation (Table 1). The extent to which current-account deficits were matched by non-debt-creating capital inflows diminished significantly. Whereas in the period 1970–73 net external borrowing could largely be used to fill up international reserves (as about 60 per cent of the annual average deficit of $10 billion was financed by official transfers and direct investment flows), this proved impossible later on. In the periods following the first oil-price shock, non-debt-creating inflows barely covered 40 per cent of capital requirements. Their share further declined to about 27 per cent at the beginning of the eighties. After 1979, development assistance in the form of outright transfers stagnated in nominal terms; the industrialised donor countries, themselves confronted by severe economic difficulties, were increasingly reluctant to grant non-repayable aid to the Third World. The record of direct investment flows was

3

Table 1: Current-Account Financing by Non-Oil Developing Countries, 1973–83 (in billions of US$)[a]

	1970–73[b]	1974–78[b]	1979	1980	1981	1982	1983[c]
Current-account deficit	10.2	37.2	61.0	89.0	107.7	86.8	67.8
Use of reserves[d]	−5.1	−8.8	−12.6	−4.5	−2.1	7.1	−7.2
Non-debt-creating flows, net	5.9	14.3	23.9	24.1	28.0	25.1	24.2
Official transfers	3.0	7.9	11.6	12.5	13.8	13.2	13.1
SDR allocations, valuation adjustments, gold monetisation	0.6	0.6	3.4	1.4	0.3	0.5	0.2
Direct investment flows, net	2.3	5.7	8.9	10.1	13.9	11.4	10.9
Net external borrowing	9.3	31.8	49.7	69.3	81.8	54.6	50.8
	(100.0)	(100.0)	(100.0)	(100.0)	(100.0)	(100.0)	(100.0)
Long-term borrowing, net	7.6	27.0	36.5	47.2	62.7	41.0	64.0
	(81.7)	(85.0)	(73.4)	(68.1)	(76.7)	(75.1)	(126.0)
From official sources	3.7	10.8	13.3	17.6	23.0	19.5	23.8
	(39.8)	(34.1)	(26.8)	(25.4)	(28.1)	(35.7)	(46.9)
From private sources	3.9	16.2	23.2	29.6	39.7	21.5	40.2
	(41.9)	(50.9)	(46.7)	(42.7)	(48.5)	(39.4)	(79.1)
Financial institutions	2.6	13.7	21.7	28.4	35.7	18.5	39.1
	(28.0)	(43.3)	(43.7)	(41.0)	(43.6)	(33.9)	(77.0)
Other lenders	1.4	2.4	1.5	1.2	4.0	3.0	1.1
	(15.1)	(7.7)	(3.0)	(1.7)	(4.9)	(5.5)	(2.2)

Table 1—continued

	1970–73[b]	1974–78[b]	1979	1980	1981	1982	1983[c]
Use of reserve-related facilities	0.1	1.9	0.4	1.8	5.9	10.7	10.8
	(1.1)	(5.9)	(0.8)	(2.6)	(7.2)	(19.6)	(21.3)
Other short-term borrowing, net, including errors and omissions	1.6	2.9	12.8	20.4	13.2	2.9	–24.1
	(17.2)	(9.1)	(25.8)	(29.4)	(16.1)	(5.3)	(–47.4)
Exceptional financing	n.a.	0.9	–0.4	4.1	6.7	14.4	–7.6
	(n.a.)	(2.7)	(0.8)	(5.9)	(8.2)	(26.4)	(–15.0)
Payment arrears	n.a.	0.4	0.8	1.1	2.4	7.1	–5.0
	(n.a.)	(1.2)	(1.6)	(1.6)	(2.9)	(13.0)	(–9.8)
Other short-term borrowing, net	1.8	6.1	14.6	20.8	10.1	–11.5	–16.5
	(19.4)	(19.3)	(29.4)	(30.0)	(12.3)	(–21.1)	(–32.5)
Residual errors and omissions	–0.2	–4.1	–1.4	–4.5	–3.7		
	(–2.2)	(–12.9)	(–2.8)	(–6.5)	(–4.5)		

[a] In parentheses: shares in net external borrowing
[b] Annual averages
[c] Projection
[d] A negative sign indicates an increase in reserves

Sources: IMF, *World Economic Outlook*; IMF, *Annual Report*.

disappointing as well, finally even resulting in a nominal
decline.

In order to restrain their external borrowing needs, many
NOPECs stopped piling up international reserves. In some
cases the use of reserves for financing deficits was probably
enforced by creditors when they hesitated or even refused to
provide additional loans. This appeared to be most evident
in 1982, when the decline in net external borrowing outpaced the reduction of current-account deficits by $6 billion.
Even in 1982, however, net borrowing remained high
compared to that in the seventies.

The international debt situation of NOPECs was also
affected by changes in the structure of credits. First, the
rising share of short-term borrowing caused concern. Taken
together, the use of reserve-related credit facilities (i.e.
credits extended by the International Monetary Fund and
short-term borrowing by monetary authorities from other
monetary authorities) and other short-term borrowing had
remained restricted to 15 per cent of total net external
borrowing, even in the period following the first oil-price
shock, whereas in the period 1979–82 it rose as high as 27
per cent. To the extent that such credits falling due for
repayment within twelve months were channelled into projects with relatively long gestation periods, debt-servicing
problems became highly probable, particularly as short-term
liabilities contributed to a bunching of maturities. Difficulties in this respect were already reflected in the 1982 figures.
Short-term lending by private sources was reduced significantly compared to the preceding three years and was
instead provided for on an involuntary basis. This is shown
by the increased amounts of payments arrears and other
forms of exceptional financing. Along with the growing risk-
awareness of private creditors and their reluctance to grant
new short-term loans, the IMF and other official monetary
authorities stepped in by greatly increasing their short-term
credit engagement in the Third World.

Second, the longer-term shift from official to private
creditors prevailing in the seventies was perceived as having
exacerbated the NOPECs' debt situation, since loans from
private sources were typically characterised by higher inter-

est rates and relatively short maturities, compared to official credits. This shift became evident not only because private short-term loans gained great importance, at least temporarily, but could also be observed with respect to long-term borrowing. As a share in total net long-term borrowing, the role of financial institutions and other private suppliers of long-term credits increased from 51 per cent between 1970 and 1973 to 60 per cent in the period 1974–78 and slightly more than 63 per cent between 1979 and 1981. In 1982 private long-term lending was reduced, relatively as well as in absolute terms, which pointed again to the commercial banks' growing risk-awareness. This is further stressed when total short-term and long-term net borrowing from private banks is added up (i.e. the sum of long-term borrowing from financial institutions, exceptional financing and other short-term borrowing in Table 1). According to a rough calculation by the IMF, private lending was estimated to have declined to some $25 billion in 1982 and $15–20 billion in 1983 compared with $52.5 billion in 1981 (although this organisation was rather optimistic in predicting a significant recovery of long-term private lending for 1983).

Extraordinarily high current-account deficits in the last decade, along with unfavourable financing patterns, nearly led to a quintupling of NOPECs' external debt outstanding in the period 1973–82 (Table 2). If long-term liabilities of OPEC countries to foreign creditors are included (amounting to $106 billion in 1982; OECD, Development Co-operation, 1982) and some OPEC short-term debt is allowed for, we end up with about $730–750 billion of external debt for all developing countries in 1982. Even on a net basis (i.e. deducting non-gold international reserves) outstanding NOPEC debt reached $535 billion. Of course, it has to be kept in mind that the tremendous nominal growth in foreign indebtedness was largely due to worldwide inflation (Solomon, 1979, p. 25 and Table 2.2; Ganoe, 1979, p. 89; for further implications, see Bacha, Díaz Alejandro, 1982, pp. 10–2). To adjust for inflationary effects, in Table 2 the nominal net debt is deflated by an index of export prices for NOPECs. The annual average growth rate in 1973–78 is then cut down from 22 per cent in nominal terms to 10 per

Table 2: External Debt of Non-Oil Developing Countries, 1973–83 (in billions of US$)

	Total nominal debt, gross	of which short-term	(in %): long-term	Total nominal debt, net of reserves	Total real debt, net of reserves
1973	130.1	14.1	85.9	95.9	95.9
1974	160.8	14.1	85.9	125.1	92.0
1975	190.8	14.3	85.7	157.5	116.7
1976	228.0	14.5	85.5	182.5	128.5
1977	278.5	15.3	84.7	219.2	133.7
1978	336.3	14.8	85.2	261.3	154.6
1979	396.9	14.8	85.2	311.9	158.3
1980	474.0	18.0	82.0	388.0	171.7
1981	555.0	18.4	81.6	471.8	219.4
1982	612.4	18.4	81.6	534.5	286.6
1983[p]	664.3	13.9	86.1	581.1	n.a.

[p] = projection

Sources: IMF, *World Economic Outlook*; IMF, *International Financial Statistics*.

cent in real terms. The latter figure is by and large in accordance with earlier developments. Similar calculations by the World Bank showed a real increase of developing countries' debt of about 9 per cent for the period 1967–73 (World Bank, 1977, p. 110).[2] However, both before and after the first oil-price shock, real growth in foreign liabilities considerably outpaced NOPECs' real growth in gross domestic product (GDP). In 1973–78 real debt rose twice as fast as GDP in constant prices.[3] This remained true for the following years also, with the exception of 1979, when NOPECs benefited from an increase in world-market prices for their exports by 17 per cent. Especially in 1981 and 1982, the increase in international debt was extraordinarily high in real terms as the continuous expansion in nominal debt coincided with a marked decline in export prices: real growth rates of 28 per cent and 22 per cent even exceeded the corresponding nominal rates. With economic growth rates falling to unprecedentedly low levels of 3 per cent in 1980 and 2 per cent in 1981 and 1982, NOPECs experienced a significant deterioration of their international debt situation in the early eighties (Table 3):

1. At the end of 1982 all NOPECs' long-term and short-
   term external debt stood at more than 140 per cent of
   their exports of goods and services in the same year.
   The debt/export ratio was about 30 percentage points
   higher than in 1973 and 1980, favourable export years
   both in terms of volume and in terms of world-market
   prices.
2. In nine years, from 1973 to 1982, external liabilities
   relative to GDP increased by 12 percentage points,
   reaching 35 per cent at the end of this period.

Table 3: Non-Oil Developing Countries' External Debt Relative to
Exports and GDP, 1973–83 (in %)

	1973	1974–78[a]	1979	1980	1981	1982	1983[P]
Debt/exports	115.4	121.8	119.2	112.9	124.9	143.3	144.4
Debt/GDP	22.4	25.4	27.5	27.6	31.0	34.7	34.7

P = projection
a Annual average

Source: IMF, *World Economic Outlook*.

Against this background, it became increasingly difficult
for NOPECs to meet their foreign debt obligations. Problems of debt-servicing deteriorated as a significant portion of
total external credits was characterised by maturities of less
than twelve months (Table 2). In many cases, the growing
amount of short-term debt required extensive and complicated rescheduling endeavours, especially when these credits were used to finance long-term projects. The shift from
official to private creditors, most evident in the seventies, as
indicated in Table 4 (although figures herein consider long-
term debt only), added further to a stiffening of average loan
conditions, as probably did the greatly enlarged role that
private financial institutions played in providing capital. In
contrast to other private creditors who (e.g. as suppliers of
export credits) may have pursued various interests other
than maximising profits out of loans[4] and, therefore, may
have granted loans at relatively modest terms, commercial
banks insisted on lending at market terms.

Table 4: Distribution of Long-Term External Debt of Non-Oil Developing Countries by Type of Creditor, 1973–83 (in %)

	1973	1974–78[a]	1979	1980	1981	1982	1983[P]
Official creditors	45.6	42.1	39.3	39.4	38.1	38.7	38.3
Private creditors	54.4	58.3	60.7	60.6	61.9	61.3	61.8
Unguaranteed debt	26.2	22.6	19.9	20.0	21.4	20.8	19.9
Guaranteed debt	28.2	35.7	40.8	40.7	40.6	40.5	41.9
Financial institutions	15.5	24.5	30.4	31.3	31.9	31.9	33.9
Other private creditors	12.7	11.2	10.3	9.4	8.7	8.6	8.0

[P] = projection
[a] Annual average

Source: IMF, *World Economic Outlook*.

With the above-mentioned developments and structural changes, it was to be expected that the increase in debt-service obligations (i.e. interest payments plus amortisations on international loans falling due) would outpace nominal growth rates of foreign debt outstanding. Regarding the 1973–82 period, debt-service payments increased annually by 22 per cent on average, whereas the corresponding growth rate for total debt stood at 18.8 per cent. Debt service was six times as high in 1982 as nine years before, although amortisation figures in Table 5 do not account for repayments of short-term loans but only for the corresponding interest payments. To the extent that short-term debt is always renewed by rolling-over (i.e. by revolving creditswith short maturities which are bound in long-term projects), or that these credits are self-financing, so to speak, because of trade relatedness, it seems justified to neglect amortisation on loans with maturities of less than twelve months. However, whereas this held true by and large for the sixties and the seventies, the process of rolling-over ceased to work automatically later on. Additionally, a growing share in short-term debt was no longer trade related but rather used to finance longer-term projects. Accordingly, it became more and more inadequate to exclude short-term amortisation in calculating total debt-service obligations. In other words, both the amortisation figures and the debt-service ratios of Table 5 have to be regarded with caution as they probably understate the NOPECs' debt-service burden, especially in the early eighties.

Table 5: Debt-Service Payments of Non-Oil Developing Countries, 1973–83 (values in billions of US$; ratios in %)

	1973	1974–78[a]	1979	1980	1981	1982	1983[P]
Total debt service	17.9	32.0	65.0	76.2	94.7	107.1	93.2
Interest payments	6.9	12.7	28.0	40.4	55.1	59.2	55.1
Amortisation	11.1	19.2	36.9	35.8	39.7	47.9	38.1
Debt service/ exports	15.9	16.0	19.0	17.6	20.4	23.9	19.3
Debt service/GDP	3.1	3.5	4.5	4.4	5.3	6.1	4.9

[P] = projection
[a] Annual average

Source: IMF, *World Economic Outlook*.

This caveat notwithstanding, debt-service ratios deteriorated considerably. In 1982 all NOPECs had to devote slightly less than a quarter of their total exports of goods and services to debt-servicing, whereas even after the first oil-price shock only about a sixth of export earnings were used in such a way. Relative to their GDP, NOPECs' debt-service payments nearly doubled in 1982 compared to the early seventies. These unfavourable developments were largely due to soaring international interest rates, which caused interest payments to jump from $7 billion in 1973 to $59 billion nine years later.[5]

The fact that debt-service obligations reached 24 per cent of NOPECs' exports and 6 per cent of their GDP does not necessarily imply that international debt is no longer manageable for them. Up to now, attempts to identify critical values of debt-service ratios indicative of *future* repayment problems have failed. The same applies to whole sets of similar indicators, or so-called early warning systems.[6] What can be concluded from the above-mentioned figures, however, is that on average the NOPECs' debt situation has

worsened significantly during the last decade, in particular in
the early eighties.

NOTES

1. In accordance with a frequently used IMF-classification, NOPECs
    include oil-exporting countries whose (net) oil exports were below
    two thirds of their total exports in 1976–78 or below 1 per cent of
    the world's total oil exports. Consequently, countries like Congo,
    Ecuador, Egypt, Gabon, Mexico and Tunisia belong to the NOPEC
    group.
2. In another World Bank publication, calculations even resulted in a
    significant decline in real growth rates of developing countries'
    debt, if the periods 1969–73 and 1973–77 are compared (World
    Bank, *World Development Report*, 1979, pp. 28–9); the way of
    deflating nominal debt figures is not specified, however.
3. For economic growth rates, *see* World Bank, *World Development
    Report*, 1983, Table 2.1.
4. In the case of suppliers' credits, the lenders may be primarily
    interested in continuous and stable trade relations with borrowers.
5. The ratio of NOPECs' interest payments to their exports of goods
    and services more than doubled from 6.1 per cent in 1973 to 13.2
    per cent in 1982; on the other hand, the corresponding amortisation
    ratio with respect to long-term debt remained at about 10 per cent
    (1973: 9.8 per cent; 1982: 10.7 per cent).
6. See, for example, Petersen, 1977; for an overview of often used
    indicators and a critical review, *see* OECD, 1974.

2   International Indebtedness of Different Developing Country Groups

It is only of limited interest to examine the Third World's international indebtedness by looking exclusively at highly aggregated figures encompassing all NOPECs. Strong differences between specific groups of developing countries and between individual borrowing economies with respect to both foreign debt outstanding and debt-service burdens are well known. Before turning to consider in more detail the situation of some important individual borrowers in international capital markets, we will shortly review both the regional distribution of debt and the debt situation of different groups of Third World borrowers.

Table 6 clearly indicates that NOPECs' foreign liabilities were highly concentrated in Latin American countries, followed by Asian economies. For the former group, the

Table 6: Distribution of Long-Term External Debt of Non-Oil Developing Countries by Analytical Group of Borrowers and by Region, 1973, 1978, 1982 (in billions of US$)

By analytical group	1973	1978	1982	By region	1973	1978	1982
Net oil exporters	20.4	61.2	108.1	Africa	14.2	42.1	67.1
Net oil importers	91.4	225.4	391.5	Asia	30.0	67.4	115.1
Major exporters of manufactures	40.8	108.1	184.3	Europe	14.5	38.2	69.2
Low-income countries	25.4	53.1	80.1	Middle East	8.7	24.7	39.3
Other net oil importers	25.2	64.2	127.1	Western Hemisphere	44.4	114.3	208.9

Source: IMF, *World Economic Outlook*.

share in all NOPECs' long-term debt increased further in the recent past, from 40 per cent in both 1973 and 1978 to 42 per

13

cent in 1982. If short-term credits were included, this shift would be even more pronounced. In the Western Hemisphere short-term financing already played a relatively important role in the seventies and was later extended much faster than in other regions. In contrast, for the latter group, the Asian borrowers, shares in all NOPECs' long-term debt fell continuously from 1973 onwards by 4 percentage points to about 23 per cent. These diverse developments for the two most heavily indebted Third World regions may be due to different factors. A first hypothesis attributes the differences to the impact of negative external shocks on the NOPECs' balance of payments position, the degree of which varies from country to country (Chapter 5). The second hypothesis stresses the relevance of the borrowers' attitudes in international capital markets and, strongly connected with it, the relevance of domestic economic policies (Chapter 6).

Developing countries in Africa, Europe and the Middle East were of only minor importance when considering their external debt from an international perspective, that is focusing on possible worldwide repercussions of NOPECs' debt problems.[1] Moreover, their shares, which for any of these three regions did not reach 15 per cent, remained comparatively stable throughout the last decade.

It is striking that in 1982 net oil exporting countries accounted for $108 billion of the $500 billion total of long-term debt.[2] Even more astonishing, this group's share went up after 1973, although the borrowing needs of net oil exporters were to be expected to decline with world-market prices for oil soaring twice in 1973/74 and 1979/80. This again hints at the role domestic policies may have played in determining the extent of external finance required to cover current-account deficits.

As regards net oil importers, Table 6 shows that the bulk of foreign loans has been granted to only ten major exporters of manufactured goods.[3] They further expanded their share in all net oil importers' debt after 1973. They were perceived as offering favourable development prospects. Consequently, private creditors were eager to intensify credit relations with most of these economies up to the recent past. A second subgroup, in Table 6 labelled as other net oil importers, comprises middle-income NOPECs mainly exporting primary commodities. This subgroup also experienced a relatively favourable credit standing in international capital markets, which was often primarily based on their resource endowment. Up to 1978 their share in total net oil importers' liabilities remained at about 28 per cent. In the early eighties, however, with the drastic fall in commodity prices, many of them were successful in compensating for lost export earnings by an intensified recourse to foreign credits; this caused their share to rise to about 33 per cent in 1982. On the other hand, the external borrowing of the large group of low-income economies including more than forty countries, whose GDP per capita did not exceed the equivalent of $350 in 1978, slackened relatively from 1973 onwards, although their external liabilities were already comparatively low in the early seventies. These NOPECs still had very limited access to world capital markets because of their economic backwardness. Instead, they heavily depended on development assistance extended by industrial countries and international organisations. No doubt important donor countries decided to concentrate their aid on the poorest recipients (especially in the form of outright grants) and provided for some debt relief, thereby reducing borrowing needs of the low-income group. But the growing demand for soft loans was not met. Experiencing severe economic problems of their own, industrial countries became increasingly reluctant to expand development assistance.

Regarding the structure of foreign liabilities, differences between NOPEC subgroups are stressed once again (Table 7). Private creditors were deeply engaged in the more advanced developing countries. Their share in total long-term debt was particularly high in the case of major exporters of manufactured goods, further rising in the seventies and early eighties. Though at a somewhat lower level, countries exporting mainly oil or non-oil primary commodities, most of them falling in the middle-income range, also had strong credit relations with private lenders. However, for those economies classified as other net oil importers, the relative expansion of loans from private sources was sharply interrupted at the beginning of the

Table 7: External Debt Structure of Non-Oil Developing Countries by Analytical Group of Borrowers and by Region, 1973, 1978, 1982 (in %)[a]

By analytical group	1973	1978	1982	By region	1973	1978	1982
Net oil exporters				Africa			
Short-term debt	11.8	11.6	22.4	Short-term debt	2.7	2.5	11.0
Private creditors	69.0	64.4	69.3	Private creditors	50.7	53.8	44.1
Major exporters of manufactures				Asia			
Short-term debt	15.2	13.6	23.3	Short-term debt	11.4	13.6	18.5
Private creditors	74.0	76.0	79.4	Private creditors	25.3	37.2	43.1
Low-income countries				Europe			
Short-term debt	2.3	5.9	5.2	Short-term debt	29.2	28.4	14.3
Private creditors	13.7	22.0	17.2	Private creditors	58.6	63.6	66.5
Other net oil importers				Middle East			
Short-term debt	23.5	24.9	14.2	Short-term debt	8.3	8.4	13.0
Private creditors	52.0	55.8	55.9	Private creditors	46.0	29.0	28.8
				Western Hemisphere			
				Short-term debt	14.2	15.3	22.6
				Private creditors	75.2	78.6	81.3

[a] Short-term debt as a share in total debt outstanding; long-term debt owed to private creditors as a share in total long-term debt outstanding.

Source: IMF, *World Economic Outlook*.

eighties. With the drop in commodity prices, borrowing from official sources gathered momentum, probably to a large extent via recourse to financing schemes compensating for export shortfalls.[4] This contributed not only to the relative decline of debt owed to private creditors but might also have helped to significantly reduce the role of short-term borrowing, which throughout the seventies amounted to little less than a quarter of total debt outstanding. On the other hand, the relative importance of short-term liabilities soared by 10 percentage points for both net oil exporters and major exporters of manufactures, thereby exacerbating the debt situation for these subgroups. For low-income NOPECs the role of both private creditors and short-term loans remained negligible throughout the entire period under consideration, pointing to a rather favourable debt structure in terms of maturities and interest rates charged.

Not only with respect to the amount and growth of international indebtedness but also considering the structure of foreign liabilities, the Latin American economies proved to be the debtor countries of principal concern. The share of private creditors in total long-term borrowing by far outpaced the corresponding ratios for all other regions. Furthermore, in 1982 the Western Hemisphere most heavily relied on short-term credits which have particularly piled up in the early eighties.

The exceptional debt situation of Latin America is again reflected in Tables 8 and 9. Both (long-term and short-term) debt outstanding and debt-service payments relative to exports of goods and services were extraordinarily high.[5] Whereas the average debt/export ratio for all NOPECs amounted to 143 per cent in 1982, the corresponding figure stood at 246 per cent for the Western Hemisphere. Differences with respect to the debt-service ratio were even more pronounced. In 1982 all NOPECs had to devote less than a quarter of their export earnings to interest and amortisation payments on foreign loans; in the Western Hemisphere, however, more than 50 per cent of export earnings was thus spent. It was only relative to GDP that Latin America's debt position was comparable to the average of all non-oil Third World borrowers.

Compared to the second largest borrowing region (i.e. Asia), differences were significant even with respect to the debt/GDP ratio. In 1982 it was 11.5 percentage points higher for the Western Hemisphere, against a divergency of only 3.3 percentage points nine years before. Relative to exports, Latin America's foreign liabilities exceeded three-fold the amount for Asia; whereas, for the former region this

Table 8: Non-Oil Developing Countries' External Debt Relative to Exports and GDP by Analytical Group of Borrowers and by Region, 1973, 1978, 1982 (in %)

By analytical group	1973	1978	1982	By region	1973	1978	1982
Net oil exporters				Africa			
Debt/exports	154.7	176.9	179.5	Debt/exports	71.5	111.4	147.4
Debt/GDP	26.2	39.3	44.7	Debt/GDP	19.4	29.4	35.2
Major exporters of manufactures				Asia			
Debt/exports	91.7	101.1	116.2	Debt/exports	92.9	77.7	80.9
Debt/GDP	20.2	25.1	33.2	Debt/GDP	19.7	22.3	26.7
Low-income countries				Europe			
Debt/exports	227.9	226.3	254.1	Debt/exports	102.4	136.4	129.6
Debt/GDP	20.1	24.0	26.2	Debt/GDP	24.5	28.6	34.7
Other net oil importers				Middle East			
Debt/exports	96.9	124.8	138.0	Debt/exports	145.4	142.4	134.3
Debt/GDP	26.2	31.5	35.8	Debt/GDP	36.2	48.3	50.3
				Western Hemisphere			
				Debt/exports	176.2	211.5	245.6
				Debt/GDP	23.0	30.3	38.2

Source: IMF, *World Economic Outlook*.

Table 9: Non-Oil Developing Countries' Debt-Service Payments Relative to Exports by Analytical Group of Borrowers and by Region, 1973, 1978, 1982 (in %)

By analytical group	1973	1978	1982	By region	1973	1978	1982
Net oil exporters	29.0	34.0	37.9	Africa	8.8	12.0	20.1
Major exporters of manufactures	14.5	16.9	23.7	Asia	9.6	9.6	9.8
Low-income countries	14.6	10.3	11.8	Europe	13.5	16.3	20.5
Other net oil importers	12.7	18.2	20.5	Middle East	20.9	13.8	17.6
				Western Hemisphere	29.3	41.7	54.0

Source: IMF, *World Economic Outlook*.

indicator deteriorated considerably during the last decade, the opposite held true for the latter. Discrepancies between Latin America and Asia were most obvious with regards to debt-service obligations: as a share in exports, Asia's interest and amortisation payments on foreign loans in the early eighties amounted to only a fifth of the burden of the Western Hemisphere. This indicator remained nearly stable throughout the period under consideration in the case of Asia. On the other hand, a dramatically rising share of export earnings was absorbed by servicing external debt in Latin American economies. Differences in debt-service burden between different groups of borrowers would probably further increase if repayments on short-term loans would be included.

The critical debt-service situation in the Western Hemisphere was partly due to the huge amount of foreign debt accumulated during the seventies and early eighties. Additionally, consequences of the rather unfavourable debt structure may have come to be felt. Especially Latin American borrowers were subject to soaring international interest rates because of their strong dependence on private credit sources.[6] However, factors directly related to foreign borrowing, and often outside the control of debtor countries, might not have been solely responsible for the critical debt situation of Latin America. Though this will be discussed in greater detail in Chapters 5 and 6, the developments mentioned above already indicate that differences between NOPEC subgroups may be partly attributed to factors lying within the responsibility of Third World countries. Comparing Asia and the Western Hemisphere, it is striking that the former region was successful in expanding exports to a far greater extent than the latter.[7] The policy of stimulating and diversifying world-market sales pursued by some major Asian borrowers may have helped to avoid debt problems. First, a favourable export performance restricts the amount of foreign loans needed to finance current-account deficits. Second, it provides for a profitable utilisation of foreign debt. The risk to creditors of losing their money is reduced in this way. This, in turn, allows creditors to agree on relatively favourable loan conditions and ensures borrowers a steady inflow of external funds.

The role of export performance seems also evident when NOPECs are split into different analytical groups. Throughout the period under consideration the debt/export ratio was lowest for the major exporters of manufactured goods, notwithstanding the fact that they were hit by worldwide recession as well as by an intensified recourse to protectionism in world markets. Their debt-service burden was by and large in line with average figures for all NOPECs. Less than a quarter of total exports of goods and services was required for interest and amortisation payments in 1982, although this group no longer received development aid to a significant extent and, accordingly, depended heavily on the international capital market with its comparatively tight credit terms. On the other hand, low-income countries, in general characterised by an insufficient competitiveness in world markets, experienced extremely high debt/export ratios, in spite of rather small amounts of accumulated foreign liabilities. For them, however, the burden of servicing debt was considerably alleviated by official creditors extending soft loans and additionally granting debt relief. Due to this, the interest payments ratio for the low-income group did not exceed 5 per cent even in the early eighties, whereas the major exporters of manufactured goods had to devote 12.8 per cent of their foreign exchange earnings to interest payments in 1982.

NOTES

1. That is not to say that from the borrowing country's point of view foreign debt may not pose a major threat to further economic development. In fact, the overriding concern of both creditors in industrial countries and international organisations to prevent the Third World's indebtedness from affecting the world economy may as a consequence mean that problems of smaller borrowers will be hardly bothered about.

2. It may seem strange that some net oil exporters are to be found under the heading of non-oil developing countries. According to a reasonable classification of countries in the IMF's *World Economic*

Outlook (as in other often used statistical sources) only those countries are labelled as oil exporting economies outside the NOPEC group for which oil exports (net of any imports of crude oil) accounted for at least two-thirds of the countries' total exports and amounted to at least 100 million barrels a year, as applied to 1978–80 averages. Consequently, the following net oil exporters belonged to the NOPEC group: Bahrain, Bolivia, People's Republic of the Congo, Ecuador, Egypt, Gabon, Malaysia, Mexico, Peru, Syria, Trinidad and Tobago, and Tunisia.

3.   The classification follows the IMF system according to which this group consists of: Argentina, Brazil, Greece, Hong Kong, Israel, the Republic of Korea, Portugal, Singapore, South Africa and Yugoslavia (see for example, IMF, *World Economic Outlook*, 1983, pp. 168–9).

4.   Compensatory financing was available under the respective IMF scheme and, for member countries of the ACP-EEC arrangement (the so-called Lomé convention), under the STABEX scheme.

5.   Debt-service ratios for NOPEC subgroups are calculated in accordance with Table 5, where interest payments on short-term amortisation is disregarded.

6.   For the Western Hemisphere, interest payments relative to exports of goods and services doubled from 14.9 per cent in 1978 to 30.4 per cent four years later. For all NOPECs the corresponding ratios amounted to 7.3 per cent and 13.2 per cent, respectively. Even if compared to overall averages, in Asia both the initial level of the interest payments ratio and its increase were significantly lower (1978, 3.7 per cent; 1982, 5.7 per cent).

7.   Whereas up to the early seventies the Western Hemisphere's nominal exports were largely in line with Asian export earnings, they amounted to only two-thirds of the foreign exchange proceeds of Asian economies in 1982. Annual average growth rates in nominal terms for the period 1974–82 stood at 15.8 per cent for Asia as against 12.2 per cent for the Western Hemisphere.

3   Differences between Major Third World Borrowers

Before turning to an evaluation of external and internal factors contributing to the emergence of debt problems in Third World countries (Chs. 5 and 6), an overview of the debt situation of different NOPEC subgroups has to be supplemented by a second step of disaggregation. While looking at individual borrower countries, it is not only interesting to further analyse the differences between debtors, as we will in this chapter, but also to identify the main problem countries and to describe the debt problems they were confronted with in the early eighties, as in the chapter following.

The following analysis deals with eighteen Third World economies: Argentina, Brazil, Chile, Colombia, Egypt, India, Indonesia, the Ivory Coast, Republic of Korea, Malaysia, Mexico, Nigeria, the Philippines, Thailand, Turkey, Venezuela, Yugoslavia and Zaire.[1] What all of them have in common is that they belonged to the group of the thirty most heavily indebted developing countries at the beginning of the eighties. Taken together, the sample accounted for nearly 60 per cent of the Third World's long-term debt of $465 billion in 1980. On the other hand, the group consists of quite different economies (Table 10). Countries which were strongly dependent on energy imports are included as well as major energy exporters. Even some OPEC members—Indonesia, Nigeria and Venezuela—had accumulated considerable amounts of foreign debt.[2] This gives us the chance to test the often heard hypothesis that it was predominantly the group of oil-importing developing countries which was severely hit by external shocks in the last decade and for whom, hence, debt problems were expected to emerge first and foremost.

Besides different energy positions, the sample selected

	Population (in millions)	GDP per capita (in $)	Growth in GDP per capita (in %)	Net imports of commercial energy as percent of total consumption of commercial energy[b,c]	Net oil imports as percent of total exports[c]	Industry as percent of GDP	Exports as percent of GDP	Manufactured exports as percent of total exports
Argentina	27.7	2390	2.2	11.2	3.1	n.a.	6.9	26.4
Brazil	118.7	2050	5.1	74.0	35.1	37	8.6	37.6
Chile	11.1	2150	1.6	53.5	15.7	37	21.2	14.3
Colombia	26.7	1180	3.0	9.3	2.8	30	16.3	12.6
Egypt	39.8	580	3.4	-50.4	-25.9	35	30.3	20.3
India	673.2	240	1.4	25.9	31.7	26	7.3	60.2
Indonesia	146.6	430	4.0	-256.2	-58.9	42	30.5	2.3
Ivory Coast	8.3	1150	2.5	100.0	5.8	22	35.6	8.0
Rep. of Korea	38.2	1520	7.0	86.0	18.0	41	36.6	89.5
Malaysia	13.9	1620	4.3	-61.5	-5.5	37	59.2	18.6
Mexico	69.8	2090	2.6	-53.5	-26.2	38	12.6	11.2
Nigeria	84.7	1010	4.1	-1235.6	-87.8	42	25.7	0.2
Philippines	49.0	690	2.8	96.5	31.4	37	20.4	21.5
Thailand	47.0	670	4.7	100.0	27.4	29	24.5	22.9
Turkey	44.9	1470	3.6	61.0	58.7	30	5.0	27.4
Venezuela	14.9	3630	2.6	-297.8	-92.7	47	33.2	1.6
Yugoslavia	22.3	2620	5.4	42.6	19.7	43	24.7	72.8
Zaire	28.3	220	0.2	-12.7	3.8	23	36.1	5.1

[a] For 1980, with the exception of columns indicating growth in GDP per capita (annual averages for 1960–80), net oil imports as percent of total merchandise exports (1978), exports of goods and services as percent of GDP, and manufactured exports as percent of total merchandise exports (1980 or latest available year).

[b] Because of unallocated volumes of energy, shares are slightly distorted in some cases; for example, calculations result in shares of more than 100% for Ivory Coast and Thailand.

[c] A negative sign indicates net energy exporting countries.

Sources: World Bank, *World Development Report;* IMF, *International Financial Statistics;* UN, *Yearbook of International Trade Statistics;* UN, *Yearbook of World Energy Statistics.*

represents the wide spectrum of Third World economies with respect to factors which also may prove to be crucial in explaining divergent experiences in handling foreign debt. More advanced economies, indicated by high per capita incomes and remarkable industrialisation levels—for example, Venezuela and Yugoslavia—contrast with countries like India and Zaire, which have considerably fallen behind in terms of development levels already reached. Regarding real economic growth rates per capita for the sixties and seventies, the sample ranges from nearly stagnating borrowers—Zaire, India, Chile—to most dynamic economies like Brazil, Yugoslavia and, in particular, Korea. Probably, the two oil-price crises of 1973/74 and 1979/80 especially threatened the economic growth prospects of advanced Third World countries, whose production processes had already become relatively energy intensive (Nunnenkamp, 1982a; 1983). Furthermore, a comparatively good credit standing allowed, and possibly tempted, some of them to avoid an immediate cut in domestic absorption by an intensified borrowing in international capital markets. This, consequently, may have led to debt-servicing difficulties for these countries later on. On the other hand, it may be easier for rapidly growing economies to adjust to worsening economic conditions and, thereby, prevent the external debt situation from deteriorating.

Finally, marked differences existed with respect to the degree of world-market orientation and the sophistication and diversification of export sales. Whereas large countries such as Brazil and India—and also some economies with a smaller population like Argentina and Turkey—exported less than 10 per cent of their GDP, the corresponding shares amounted to more than 35 per cent in the cases of the Ivory Coast, Zaire, Korea and Malaysia. World-market sales of manufactured goods played a negligible role for the three OPEC members included, but such sales dominated exports from India, Yugoslavia and Korea. Again two conflicting hypotheses can be advanced. The outward-looking Third World economies were particularly vulnerable to recessionary influences from world markets; hence, it can be supposed that the slackening import demand of major industrialised trading partners affected their current-account position and increased their foreign capital requirements significantly, eventually laying foundations for future debt problems. However, this sensitivity to world-market developments notwithstanding, a diversified and internationally competitive export structure may have helped balance of payments adjustment and possibly was well-suited to reduce the foreign financing needs of borrowing countries.

Although the eighteen countries included had this in common—that they, together with only a few more Third World borrowers, constituted the group of most heavily indebted economies—the prevailing sharp differences in the extent of liabilities accumulated, even within this sample, are stressed in Table 11 (which presents data for the most recent periods and, for means of comparison, the earliest available year as well as the year preceding the first oil-price shock and the following external disturbances). In 1980, for example, the debt figures of Mexico and Brazil exceeded those of countries like Malaysia, Zaire, the Ivory Coast, Colombia, Nigeria and Thailand by a factor of between eight and fifteen. In terms of debt per capita of population, discrepancies were even more pronounced ranging from $30 and $60 in India and Nigeria to $810 and $930 in Chile and Venezuela. In this respect, the largest borrowers in absolute terms still belonged to the top group within the sample with a per capita indebtedness of $480 (Brazil) and $620 (Mexico).

Before further analysing the foreign debt situation some qualifications have to be made concerning the statistical base. Searching for country-specific data on international indebtedness, three principal sources may be referred to:

1. The Bank for International Settlements (BIS) in Basle periodically reports liabilities and assets of borrowing countries to commercial banks in the Group of Ten countries, some other industrial countries and to certain of their foreign affiliates in major offshore banking centres.[3] Short-term debt is included. The BIS does not consider debt owed to other creditors rather than commercial banks. Hence, this source is not appropriate for portraying the debt situation as completely as

Table 11: International Debt (Disbursements) of Major Third World Borrowing Countries, 1967, 1973, 1978–82[a] (in billions of US$)

	1967	1973	1978	1979	1980	1981	1982
Argentina	n.a.	n.a.	8.8	12.7	16.0	23.7	27.1
	(1.7)	(2.8)	(6.7)	(8.6)	(10.2)	(10.5)	(n.a.)
Brazil	n.a.	12.6	45.3	50.8	57.0	64.7	72.5
	(2.4)	(7.5)	(30.3)	(35.6)	(39.2)	(43.8)	(n.a.)
Chile	n.a.	3.2	5.7	7.1	9.0	11.9	13.4
	(1.0)	(2.8)	(4.4)	(4.8)	(4.7)	(4.4)	(n.a.)
Colombia	n.a.	2.3	3.3	3.9	4.6	6.0	n.a.
	(0.7)	(1.9)	(2.8)	(3.4)	(4.0)	(5.0)	(n.a.)
Egypt	n.a.	n.a.	10.4	12.2	13.8	15.0	17.5
	(1.5)[b]	(2.2)	(9.9)	(11.4)	(12.8)	(13.9)	(n.a.)
India	n.a.	10.5	15.7	16.5	18.0	18.9	20.8
	(5.0)	(10.4)	(15.4)	(15.6)	(17.4)	(17.9)	(n.a.)
Indonesia	n.a.	n.a.	14.5	15.0	16.6	17.3	19.9
	(1.9)	(5.3)	(13.1)	(13.2)	(14.9)	(15.5)	(n.a.)
Ivory Coast	n.a.	n.a.	3.0	3.8	4.5	n.a.	n.a.
	(0.2)	(0.6)	(2.8)	(3.6)	(4.3)	(4.5)	(n.a.)
Rep. of Korea	n.a.	3.8	12.7	15.5	17.6	19.6	22.0
	(0.3)	(3.5)	(11.4)	(13.9)	(16.3)	(20.0)	(n.a.)
Malaysia	n.a.	n.a.	3.1	3.5	3.9	n.a.	n.a.
	(0.2)	(0.7)	(2.5)	(2.8)	(3.1)	(4.6)	(n.a.)
Mexico	n.a.	n.a.	32.5	37.6	43.5	53.3	60.5
	(1.8)	(5.6)	(25.6)	(29.2)	(33.6)	(42.7)	(n.a.)
Nigeria	n.a.	n.a.	2.6	4.2	5.2	6.0	8.0
	(0.3)	(1.2)	(2.3)	(3.2)	(4.0)	(4.7)	(n.a.)
Philippines	n.a.	1.9	6.3	7.4	8.5	10.0	12.2
	(0.3)	(0.9)	(4.2)	(5.1)	(6.4)	(7.4)	(n.a.)
Thailand	n.a.	0.9	2.7	3.9	5.8	7.3	n.a.
	(0.2)	(0.4)	(1.8)	(2.8)	(4.1)	(5.2)	(n.a.)
Turkey	n.a.	3.0	7.3	11.6	14.5	14.5	14.9
	(1.1)	(2.9)	(6.4)	(11.0)	(13.5)	(13.8)	(n.a.)
Venezuela	n.a.	n.a.	9.4	12.3	13.8	14.9	16.7
	(0.3)	(1.5)	(6.9)	(9.8)	(10.9)	(11.4)	(n.a.)
Yugoslavia	n.a.	4.3	11.0	13.5	15.1	15.1	14.2
	(1.1)	(1.9)	(3.4)	(3.7)	(4.6)	(5.3)	(n.a.)
Zaire	n.a.	n.a.	3.6	4.2	4.2	n.a.	n.a.
	(0.3)[c]	(0.9)	(3.6)	(3.8)	(3.8)	(4.0)	(n.a.)

[a] Private non-guaranteed debt included as far as possible; in parentheses: public and publicly guaranteed debt.
[b] 1968.
[c] 1969.

Sources: OECD, *Development Co-operation*; OECD, *External Debt of Developing Countries*; World Bank, *World Debt Tables*.

possible.[4]

2. The World Bank's World Debt Tables provide for time-series data on international debt back to the sixties which, additionally, give rather detailed insights. There are some severe limitations, however. Besides neglecting short-term liabilities and not accounting for borrowers' foreign assets, it is most important that, for many countries, only public and publicly guaranteed debt is presented. Especially for borrowers like Mexico which piled up considerable amounts of private non-guaranteed liabilities, the World Bank figures heavily underestimate the actual degree of indebtedness. Consequently, this source is only used as a supplement, mainly to inform about developments in the late sixties and early seventies (see figures in parentheses in Table 11).

3. The third source—statistics compiled by the Organisation for Economic Co-operation and Development (OECD)—has some deficiencies in common with the World Debt Tables. Data are on a gross basis and exclude short-term loans as well as military debt financed by official credits and debt owed to the IMF.[5] Moreover, consistent time series reach only back to the mid-seventies. On the other hand, data are presented with comparatively short delay, at least on a preliminary basis. In contrast to the World Bank, the OECD, in principle, covers both public and private debt, whether guaranteed or not.[6] Because of these two strong advantages, OECD statistics are relied upon in this chapter whenever available.

Table 11 clearly indicates that, in many cases, it would be strongly misleading to deal with public and publicly guaranteed debt exclusively. The most impressive examples in this respect were Yugoslavia and Chile, where non-guaranteed liabilities amounted to roughly two-thirds of total debt in the early eighties, followed by Argentina and Brazil with corresponding shares of 56 per cent and 32 per cent. For seven more sample countries public and publicly guaranteed debt was about 20 per cent lower than total figures. Apparently, however, due to remaining data limitations even total debt figures of Table 11 often considerably understate the actual gross debt burden. Estimates published by Morgan Guaranty Trust for most of our sample countries (Table 12) resulted in gross external debt figures for 1982 which exceeded the corresponding OECD figures by 37 per cent on an average. Extraordinarily high discrepancies emerged for Venezuela (77 per cent), Korea (64 per cent) and Turkey (53 per cent). These deviations are presumably mainly due to short-term liabilities which are accounted for in Table 12 only. Additionally, the principal reporting systems used by the OECD seem to fail in drawing a complete picture on long-term debt in some cases.

Another factor causing distortions in time series data remains to be mentioned, though its influence was only of minor importance for the Third World as a whole.[7] All external liabilities of developing country borrowers are expressed in US dollars, but only about one-half of their total debt is denominated in this currency (OECD, 1982, p. 49). An appreciation (depreciation) of the US dollar reduces (increases) the dollar value of the non-dollar denominated liabilities. Accordingly, exchange-rate fluctuations in the past resulted in an overstatement of actual increases in foreign debt in the late seventies (when the dollar depreciated). This development was reversed later when the dollar strengthened its position again. In 1981 the impact of exchange-rate variations caused the developing countries' debt burden, as expressed in US dollars, to be understated by 7.4 per cent, according to an OECD estimate. In the following period the distortion in the same direction was probably even slightly higher.

Regarding the growth rates in international debt of Table 13, the above-mentioned limitations have to be borne in mind. Up to 1980, the sample countries, on an average, experienced an average annual increase in foreign liabilities of about 20 per cent in nominal terms (according to OECD and World Bank data). There were only minor changes in nominal growth rates for sub-periods 1967–73, 1973–78 and 1978–80.[8] In real terms, that is, adjusted for export price variations on the borrowers' side, growth rates were roughly halved to between 10 and 12 per cent, both before and after

Table 12: Total External Debt and Debt-Service Obligations of Some Major Third World Borrowing Countries

	Gross external debt at end-1982[a] (in billions of US$)	Debt service in 1983 as percent of exports[b]	
		Total[c]	Excluding roll-over of short-term debt
Argentina	38.0	154	88
Brazil	85.5	117	67
Chile	17.2	104	54
Colombia	10.3	95	38
Egypt	19.2	46	16
Indonesia	25.4	28	14
Ivory Coast	9.2	76	34
Rep. of Korea	36.0	49	17
Malaysia	10.4	15	7
Mexico	80.1	126	59
Nigeria	9.3	28	14
Philippines	16.6	79	33
Thailand	11.0	50	19
Turkey	22.8	65	20
Venezuela	29.5	101	25

[a] Short-term debt included.
[b] Debt service as percent of exports of goods and services, including net private transfer payments.
[c] Interest and amortisation of short-term debt included.

Source: Morgan Guaranty Trust, *World Financial Markets.*

Table 13: Nominal and Real Growth of International Debt of Major Third World Borrowing Countries,[a] 1967–82 (in percent)

	1967–73		1973–78		1978–80		1980–81		1981–82	
	nominal	real	nominal	real	nominal	real	nominal	real	nominal	real
Argentina	n.a.	n.a.	n.a.	n.a.	34.8	11.8	48.1	54.4	14.3	n.a.
	(8.7)	(−1.5)	(19.1)	(18.8)	(23.4)	(2.5)	(2.9)	(6.9)	(n.a.)	(n.a.)
Brazil	n.a.	n.a.	29.2	17.1	12.2	4.0	13.5	20.7	12.1	18.6
	(20.9)	(10.5)	(32.2)	(19.9)	(13.7)	(5.5)	(11.7)	(18.6)	(n.a.)	(n.a.)
Chile	n.a.	n.a.	12.2	14.1	25.7	2.9	32.2	50.0	12.6	n.a.
	(18.7)	(9.2)	(9.5)	(11.1)	(3.4)	(−15.6)	(−6.4)	(6.4)	(n.a.)	(n.a.)
Colombia	n.a.	n.a.	7.5	−9.7	18.1	13.0	30.4	45.7	n.a.	n.a.
	(18.1)	(8.3)	(8.1)	(−9.1)	(19.5)	(13.6)	(25.0)	(40.0)	(n.a.)	(n.a.)
Egypt	n.a.	n.a.	n.a.	n.a.	15.2	−4.4	8.7	5.8	16.7	n.a.
	(8.0) [b]	(0.7) [b]	(35.1)	(20.6)	(13.7)	(−5.4)	(8.6)	(5.5)	(n.a.)	(n.a.)
India	n.a.	n.a.	8.4	−1.1	7.1	−3.2	5.0	n.a.	10.1	n.a.
	(13.0)	(7.5)	(8.2)	(−1.3)	(6.3)	(−3.8)	(2.9)	(n.a.)	(n.a.)	(n.a.)
Indonesia	n.a.	n.a.	n.a.	n.a.	7.0	−25.4	4.2	4.2	15.0	n.a.
	(18.6)	(−3.0)	(19.8)	(−2.1)	(6.6)	(−25.6)	(4.0)	(4.0)	(n.a.)	(n.a.)
Ivory Coast	n.a.	n.a.	n.a.	n.a.	22.5	10.3	n.a.	n.a.	n.a.	n.a.
	(20.1)	(n.a.)	(36.1)	(16.3)	(23.9)	(12.5)	(4.7)	(41.9)	(n.a.)	(n.a.)
Republic of Korea	n.a.	n.a.	27.3	16.1	17.7	4.9	11.4	8.5	12.2	17.3
	(50.6)	(43.5)	(26.6)	(15.4)	(19.6)	(6.8)	(22.7)	(19.6)	(n.a.)	(n.a.)
Malaysia	n.a.	n.a.	n.a.	n.a.	12.2	−12.6	n.a.	n.a.	n.a.	n.a.
	(23.2)	(15.2)	(29.0)	(14.3)	(11.4)	(−13.0)	(48.4)	(61.3)	(n.a.)	(n.a.)
Mexico	n.a.	n.a.	n.a.	n.a.	15.7	−1.1	22.5	37.7	13.5	n.a.
	(20.8)	(11.5)	(35.5)	(24.2)	(14.6)	(−2.2)	(27.1)	(42.9)	(n.a.)	(n.a.)
Nigeria	n.a.	n.a.	n.a.	n.a.	41.4	−11.3	15.4	5.8	33.3	45.5
	(26.0)	(11.1)	(13.9)	(−11.5)	(31.9)	(−17.0)	(17.5)	(7.5)	(n.a.)	(n.a.)
Philippines	n.a.	n.a.	27.1	20.4	16.2	2.4	17.6	20.0	22.0	47.1
	(20.1)	(13.5)	(36.1)	(29.2)	(23.4)	(8.9)	(15.6)	(18.8)	(n.a.)	(n.a.)
Thailand	n.a.	n.a.	24.6	16.1	46.6	23.5	25.9	34.5	n.a.	n.a.
	(12.2)	(4.9)	(35.1)	(25.6)	(50.9)	(28.1)	(26.8)	(34.1)	(n.a.)	(n.a.)
Turkey	n.a.	n.a.	19.5	9.2	40.9	19.8	0.0	12.4	2.8	10.4
	(17.5)	(n.a.)	(17.2)	(7.2)	(45.2)	(23.2)	(2.2)	(14.8)	(n.a.)	(n.a.)
Venezuela	n.a.	n.a.	n.a.	n.a.	21.2	−18.7	8.0	−7.2	12.1	12.5
	(30.8)	(17.8)	(35.7)	(5.9)	(25.7)	(−15.6)	(4.6)	(−10.1)	(n.a.)	(n.a.)
Yugoslavia	n.a.	n.a.	20.7	7.2	17.2	−0.7	0.0	n.a.	−6.0	n.a.
	(9.5)	(2.7)	(12.3)	(−0.4)	(16.3)	(−1.1)	(15.2)	(n.a.)	(n.a.)	(n.a.)
Zaire	n.a.	n.a.	n.a.	n.a.	8.0	−7.4	n.a.	n.a.	n.a.	n.a.
	(31.6) [c]	(23.6) [c]	(32.0)	(28.5)	(2.7)	(−11.9)	(5.3)	(26.3)	(n.a.)	(n.a.)

[a] In parentheses: Growth rates for public and publicly guaranteed debt only.

[b] 1968–73.

[c] 1969–73.

Sources: Table 11; IMF, *International Financial Statistics*; UNCTAD, *Handbook of International Trade and Development Statistics*.

the first oil-price shock of 1973/74. Parallel to the second drastic rise in petroleum prices, real international debt remained nearly constant in 1978–80.[9] This, of course, was largely due to the five sample countries for which oil exports contributed significantly to foreign exchange earnings. For

Egypt, Indonesia, Mexico, Nigeria and Venezuela, export prices, on an average, soared by more than 90 per cent from 1978 to 1980. But also the other debtors benefited from improved world-market conditions. Their export prices rose by 34 per cent.

However, this rather favourable picture was turned upside down only shortly afterwards. Whereas the nominal increase in foreign debt was reduced in the early eighties to between 13 and 16 per cent (approx.), real growth rates exploded in spite of this, reaching 23 per cent and 25 per cent in 1981 and 1982, respectively, as export prices fell sharply.[10] In this context it must be stressed that the remarkable shift in real growth of developing countries' debt in the recent past was probably even more pronounced than reflected in figures of Table 13, because of the data shortcomings discussed above. Most important, all major qualifications pointed in the same direction; that is, further aggravating the debt situation after 1980. Short-term loans gained significantly in importance; hence, not only the overall level of indebtedness is understated but also the increase in foreign liabilities when calculated on the basis of credits with maturities of more than one year exclusively. In addition, the US dollar continued to appreciate, which again distorted debt figures on the lower side.

The development of the Third World countries' debt situation in the early eighties was furthermore affected when looked at on a net basis (i.e. deducting foreign reserves from gross debt figures). Table 14 shows that the extent to which debtor countries piled up non-gold reserves slowed down drastically. In many cases, reserves were even partly exhausted in order to reduce the need for fresh money from international capital markets. The negative impact of changed policies with respect to reserves on net indebtedness peaked in the recent past: in 1978 and 1980, international non-gold reserves in eleven and ten cases, respectively, out of eighteen borrowers exceeded one-fifth of their total long-term debt. Later on the number of countries reaching this level dwindled to eight out of fifteen (1981), and only three out of thirteen debtors (1982) for which the data set allowed continuing calculations. Consequently, the dis-

Table 14: International Non-Gold Reserves of Major Third World Borrowing Countries, 1973–82 (in billions of US$)

	1973	1978	1979	1980	1981	1982
Argentina	1.2	5.0	9.4	6.8	3.3	2.5
Brazil	6.4	11.9	9.0	5.7	6.6	4.0
Chile	0.1	1.0	2.0	3.1	3.3	1.8
Colombia	0.5	2.3	3.8	4.8	4.8	3.9
Egypt	0.2	0.5	0.5	1.0	0.7	0.7
India	0.8	6.4	7.4	6.9	4.7	4.3
Indonesia	0.8	2.6	4.1	5.4	5.0	3.2
Ivory Coast	0.1	0.4	0.1	0.0	0.0	0.0
Republic of Korea	0.8	2.7	2.9	2.9	2.7	2.8
Malaysia	1.3	3.3	4.0	4.3	4.1	3.8
Mexico	1.2	1.8	2.1	2.9	4.1	0.9
Nigeria	0.6	1.8	5.5	10.2	3.8	1.7
Philippines	1.0	1.8	2.2	2.8	2.2	1.8
Thailand	1.2	2.0	1.8	1.5	1.7	1.5
Turkey	1.9	0.8	0.8	1.3	1.3	0.9
Venezuela	1.9	6.0	7.4	6.6	8.1	6.6
Yugoslavia	1.3	2.3	1.3	1.4	1.6	0.8
Zaire	0.1	0.1	0.3	0.3	0.1	0.1

Source: IMF, *International Financial Statistics*.

crepancy in real growth rates between the seventies and the early eighties, observed already when discussing gross figures, is further enlarged on a net basis. Whereas in the seventies net real growth rates were only slightly higher than gross real growth rates for total debt in Table 13, they later on exceeded gross figures by more than 10 percentage points.[11]

Concentrating on the years following the first oil-price shock, it was only in the case of Thailand that debt growth-rates continuously and considerably (i.e. by more than 5 percentage points) exceeded average figures for all eighteen borrowers included, both in nominal as well as in real terms (Table 13). In the period 1973–78, the foreign liabilities of Brazil, Egypt, Mexico, the Philippines, Zaire and, to a somewhat lesser extent, for Korea, Argentina (in real terms only), the Ivory Coast and Venezuela (both in nominal terms only) also increased much faster than on an average. In course of time, however, there was some fluctuation in the top group with respect to growth in external debt. In 1978–81, only Argentina, Thailand and the Ivory Coast (in real terms) stayed there, whereas Mexico reappeared at the top again in 1981. As a new member Turkey joined this group for the late seventies, as did Nigeria (in nominal terms) and Colombia (in real terms). Colombia remained there in 1981, when also Chile, Malaysia and Zaire (in real terms only) experienced growth rates significantly above the average.[12] In other words, only India, Indonesia and Yugoslavia never appeared in the group of borrowers whose indebtedness mounted most rapidly. This picture does not change significantly when growth rates for individual debtors are calculated after netting out international non-gold reserves. With regard to real increases in long-term debt, the classification of being a member of the top group or not has to be substantially revised in only five out of the possible forty cases.[13]

NOTES

1. In contrast to Chapters 1 and 2, the following analysis is not restricted to NOPECs (see also note 1 of Chapter 1). The sample includes three OPEC countries (Indonesia, Nigeria, Venezuela). For an explanation, see the text.
2. Liabilities were sometimes largely matched by the borrowing countries' own assets in international capital markets in these cases. This held true, too, for Iran, Saudi Arabia and, to a lesser extent, for Algeria, which also belonged to the group of most heavily indebted developing countries if ranked according to gross debt figures in 1980. When accounting for foreign assets, at least Saudi Arabia turned out to be an important net lender in international capital markets.
3. The Group of Ten consists of Belgium and Luxemburg, Canada, France, Federal Republic of Germany, Italy, Japan, Netherlands, Sweden, United Kingdom and United States. Additionally, the external positions of banks in Austria, Denmark, Ireland and Switzerland are accounted for. The two most important periodically published BIS sources are *International Banking Developments* and *The Maturity Structure of International Bank Lending*.
4. The BIS publications will be referred to, however, in Chapter 7, which deals with the lending attitudes of commercial banks in the last decade.

5 Military debt financed by official credits for NOPEC countries as a whole is estimated to represent some 10 per cent of total reported debt in 1981. Debt to the IMF (other than to the IMF Trust Fund which is included in reported figures) amounted to about $9.5 billion at the end of 1980 for all NOPECs and $14.9 billion at the end of 1981 (OECD, 1982, p. 46).

6. For a detailed description of coverage and sources of the OECD's external debt statistics, *see* OECD, 1982, p. 46–9.

7. For individual debtor countries the impact can differ widely from the overall impact. Country-specific calculations, however, are not available.

8. The unweighted average growth rates for the eighteen debtor countries amounted to 20.5 per cent in 1967–73 (for public and publicly guaranteed debt only), 19.6 per cent (for total debt) and 24.5 per cent (for public and publicly guaranteed debt) in 1973–78, and 21.1 per cent and 19.6 per cent, respectively, in 1978–80.

9. For total debt, the annual increase stood at only 0.4 per cent; calculations for public and publicly guaranteed debt even resulted in an annual average decline of 0.6 per cent.

10. Those non-oil exporters for whom data were available up to 1982 (eight countries out of thirteen) suffered a 17 per cent decline in export prices within two years; four of the remaining five economies of this subgroup (data for Yugoslavia were not available for later than 1980) experienced on an average a fall of 9 per cent in 1981 only. Even for Mexico as an important oil exporter the loss in export prices amounted to 11 per cent in 1981. With regard to real growth rates of external debt for 1981 and 1982 given in the text, it has to be recalled that due to data limitations the number of countries for which averages can be calculated is reduced to thirteen (1981) and only six (1982).

11. For the period 1973–78 the discrepancy amounted to 1.3 percentage points (9.9 per cent growth on a gross basis; 11.2 per cent net). In the early eighties the difference was 10.3 percentage points (22.5 per cent versus 32.8 per cent in 1980–81) and 11.9 percentage points (21.2 per cent versus 33.1 per cent in 1981–82 when disregarding Nigeria; otherwise the difference would be considerably higher).

12. For 1982 a comparison would be meaningless because the sample is strongly diminished due to non-availability of data.

13. For the following cases the classification clearly changes: Turkey in 1973–78 and Brazil in 1978–80 (both joining the top group on a net basis in the periods indicated), Colombia in 1978–80 (leaving the top group), the Philippines in 1980–81 and Venezuela in 1981–82 (as new members at the top).

Part II
THE CAUSES

4   Identifying Problem Borrowers

Focusing on those sample countries which at least in two of the three periods 1973–78, 1978–80 and 1980–81 experienced extraordinarily high increases in indebtedness, we come up with eight borrowers (on a net basis, i.e. if adjustments required by variations in international reserves are accounted for; see pp. 31–3): Argentina, Brazil, the Ivory Coast, Mexico, the Philippines, Thailand, Turkey and Zaire. The question now arises whether these countries can be considered as problem countries in the sense that foreign debt was no longer manageable for them. Problem borrowers may be defined as being unable to meet their interest and amortisation obligations as mutually agreed upon originally. It may suffice, however, that foreign lenders are afraid that this will happen in future and hence refuse to provide fresh capital and, possibly, even interrupt the rollover process. Doubts on the lenders' side about the creditworthiness of borrowers by themselves may—as a self-fulfilling prophecy—cause a country to become a problem borrower, which then may further affect the smooth functioning of international financial markets. With the renewal of credits declined, otherwise profitable projects may fail, causing payment tensions which are only the result of the lenders' distrust.

It may be argued that an extensive or even excessive growth in the indebtedness of the eight borrowers listed above made future difficulties in servicing foreign credits highly probable. Growth rates as an indicator of arising debt problems are insufficient, however, and may be clearly misleading. The increase took place on quite different levels of international debt accumulated up to 1973. For example, Brazil and Mexico then owed about ten to twenty times the amount of public and publicly guaranteed loans to foreign creditors of Thailand and the Ivory Coast. Additionally, the major role of credits from private sources (especially those which were not publicly guaranteed) in countries like Argentina and Brazil probably made debt-servicing as scheduled more difficult to achieve than, for example, for the Ivory Coast, where the debt structure rather alleviated the debt burden. Still more important, countries differed widely in terms of GDP and export growth. With respect to the former, Mexico, the Philippines and Thailand experienced impressive real annual average growth rates of 6.2, 4.6 and 5.6 per cent in 1978–82, whereas Zaire (1.7 per cent annually in 1978–81) and, in particular, Argentina (−1 per cent in 1978–82) were on the negative side. Regarding the latter (i.e. growth in export proceeds), annual average figures ranged from 38 per cent in Mexico and 26 per cent in Turkey to −0.2 per cent in the Ivory Coast and −11.4 per cent in Zaire (all rates for 1978–82). Hence, though commonly characterised by a rapidly increasing indebtedness, the eight borrowers offered rather contrasting prospects for servicing loans on the basis of a parallel increase in domestic economic activity and foreign exchange earned through exports.

Part of the inadequacy in using growth rates in indebtedness as an indicator for identifying problem countries may be avoided by referring to debt-service ratios. While focusing on debt service, adjustment is made for the impact the structural composition of liabilities exerts on the debt burden. By calculating ratios, the borrowers' economic potential to meet debt-service obligations is accounted for. Most frequently, interest and amortisation payments are considered relative to the country's exports (DS/E) and to its GDP (DS/GDP). With regard to the DS/E ratio, Table 15 indicates that as early as 1980 three countries—Brazil, Mexico, Egypt—had to devote more than half of their merchandise exports to servicing foreign loans (non-guaranteed credits included). They were followed by Chile, Turkey, Yugoslavia and Argentina, for which ratios amounted to between 48 and 35 per cent. At the other end stood countries like Malaysia, Nigeria and Indonesia, where interest and amortisation payments absorbed less than 10 per cent of earnings from world-market sales.[1] Chile, Egypt, Yugoslavia, Brazil and Mexico also experienced an extra-

Table 15: Debt-Service Ratios for Major Third World Borrowing Countries, 1973, 1978–82[a] (in percent)

		1973	1978	1979	1980	1981	1982
Argentina	DS/E	n.a.	40.2	26.6	35.0	48.1	82.6
	DS/GDP	n.a.	3.9	2.0	1.8	3.6	n.a.
Brazil	DS/E	n.a.	66.2	74.9	66.1	65.7	90.7
	DS/GDP	n.a.	4.1	4.9	5.3	5.3	n.a.
Chile	DS/E	n.a.	58.9	44.7	47.5	76.8	62.8
	DS/GDP	n.a.	9.5	8.4	8.1	9.1	10.0
Colombia	DS/E	27.2	16.3	22.4	15.5	38.9	n.a.
	DS/GDP	3.1	2.1	2.6	1.8	3.1	n.a.
Egypt	DS/E	n.a.	73.1	69.6	52.5	71.1	80.1
	DS/GDP	n.a.	5.1	7.2	6.7	7.9	7.9
India	DS/E	26.1	15.9	14.6	16.6	19.2	n.a.
	DS/GDP	1.0	0.9	0.9	0.8	0.8	n.a.
Indonesia	DS/E	n.a.	16.1	14.4	9.6	11.2	17.2
	DS/GDP	n.a.	3.6	4.4	2.9	2.9	n.a.
Ivory Coast	DS/E	n.a.	22.0	26.7	28.6	n.a.	n.a.
	DS/GDP	n.a.	6.5	7.4	n.a.	n.a.	n.a.
Republic of Korea	DS/E	20.5	15.7	19.5	19.0	18.3	21.1
	DS/GDP	5.0	4.2	4.8	5.7	6.0	6.7
Malaysia	DS/E	n.a.	10.9	5.7	3.9	n.a.	n.a.
	DS/GDP	n.a.	5.2	3.1	2.1	n.a.	n.a.
Mexico	DS/E	n.a.	119.2	127.4	61.7	55.2	60.2
	DS/GDP	n.a.	6.9	8.5	5.2	4.5	7.7
Nigeria	DS/E	n.a.	6.1	4.4	4.5	9.2	12.8
	DS/GDP	n.a.	1.4	1.2	1.5	2.5	n.a.
Philippines	DS/E	24.9	34.7	29.1	18.6	28.3	38.2
	DS/GDP	4.4	4.9	4.4	3.0	4.1	4.8
Thailand	DS/E	n.a.	19.8	18.3	18.8	18.8	n.a.
	DS/GDP	n.a.	3.5	3.6	3.6	3.7	n.a.
Turkey	DS/E	20.5	25.8	40.2	39.2	27.7	40.0
	DS/GDP	1.3	1.1	1.3	2.0	2.3	4.4
Venezuela	DS/E	n.a.	17.0	19.3	24.6	24.8	27.8
	DS/GDP	n.a.	3.9	5.7	7.9	7.4	7.5
Yugoslavia	DS/E	31.9	33.9	42.2	37.2	31.1	35.0
	DS/GDP	4.9	4.0	4.5	5.4	5.5	n.a.
Zaire	DS/E	n.a.	21.6	18.1	28.8	n.a.	n.a.
	DS/GDP	n.a.	3.0	3.8	7.7	n.a.	n.a.

[a] DS/E: Debt service on long-term debt (non-guaranteed debt included as far as possible) as percent of merchandise exports.
DS/GDP: Debt service on long-term debt (non-guaranteed debt included as far as possible) as percent of gross domestic product.

Sources: OECD, *Development Co-operation*; OECD, *External Debt of Developing Countries*; World Bank, *World Debt Tables*; IMF, *International Financial Statistics*.

ordinarily high debt service relative to their GDP. In 1980 the DS/GDP ratio exceeded 5 per cent for them, as, additionally, for Venezuela, Zaire and Korea.

Taking both indicators together, the relative debt-service burden in 1980 was most heavily felt in Chile, Egypt, Brazil, Mexico, Zaire, Venezuela, Yugoslavia and Korea (in descending order of average rank positions), whereas it was rather modest in the Philippines, Indonesia, Colombia, Malaysia, India and Nigeria—the other borrowers lying in-between. For only three out of the eight members of the top group—Brazil, Mexico and Zaire—the increase in total indebtedness as presented above was especially high, which again hints at the inadequacy of calculating growth rates in international debt as an indicator for the economic burden which sprang from foreign loans. In the case of the Philippines, a fast growing indebtedness even went hand in hand with rather low debt-service ratios.[2]

For Venezuela, Zaire, Korea and Brazil the debt-service situation was further aggravated in so far as they not only appeared in the group with the highest ratios in 1980 but, additionally, ratios on an average deteriorated most remarkably for them from 1978 to the early eighties.[3] A significant worsening in ratios has also to be reported for Nigeria, Colombia, Turkey and Argentina. Especially for Nigeria and Colombia, however, this unfavourable development started from very low indicator levels.

The borrowers which according to the level and the increase in debt-service ratios might be expected to run into difficulties first of all, might also be regarded as the trouble-makers if a more comprehensive indicator system is constructed. The procedure is as follows: the eighteen sample countries were ranked with respect to each out of ten indicators (Table 16), whereby rank one (eighteen) always identifies the country in the worst (best) position.[4] Calculating the average rank positions for all ten indicators, the foreign debt situation was tightest for Turkey, Chile and Brazil, where average ranks were found to be between 6.2 and 6.8. The next group consisted of Egypt, Argentina and Mexico, with average rank positions of between 7.1 and 7.9, closely followed by the Ivory Coast (8.0), Korea (8.3) and Venezuela (8.4). Two more countries experienced average rank positions considerably below ten—Zaire, 8.8 and Yugoslavia, 9.1— whereas for the remaining debtor coun-

Table 16: Ranking of Major Third World Borrowing Countries with Respect to Different Indicators[a]

	Debt outstanding in 1980	Debt per capita in 1980	Debt as percent of GDP in 1980	Debt as percent of merchandise exports in 1980	Debt service as percent of GDP in 1980	Debt service as percent of merchandise exports in 1980	Nominal increase in debt 1978–82[b]	Real increase in debt 1978–81[b]	Change in debt service as percent of GDP in 1978–81[b]	Change in debt service as percent of merchandise exports 1978–82[b]
Argentina	6	5	17	7	15.5	7	2	2	13	3
Brazil	1	7	11.5	3	8	1	13	8	9	6
Chile	11	2	4	8	1	4	4	5	12	13.5
Colombia	15	12.5	15	13	15.5	15	6	3	6	1
Egypt	9.5	9	2	2	5	3	12	12	5	11.5
India	3	18	16	6	18	14	17	13	14	10
Indonesia	5	16	11.5	16	12	16	15	18	16	13.5
Ivory Coast	16	6	3	11	4	9	5	7	10	9
Rep. of Korea	4	8	5	14	6	11	11	10	7	7
Malaysia	18	11	14	12	13	18	14	16	18	18
Mexico	2	4	9	4	9	2	9	6	17	17
Nigeria	14	17	18	18	17	17	3	14	4	2
Philippines	12	12.5	8	10	11	13	8	9	15	11.5
Thailand	13	15	13	15	10	12	1	1	11	16
Turkey	8	10	6	1	14	5	7	4	2	5
Venezuela	9.5	1	10	17	2	10	10	17	3	4
Yugoslavia	7	3	7	9	7	6	18	11	8	15
Zaire	17	14	1	5	3	8	16	15	1	8

[a] Rank 1 always indicates the country in the most unfavourable position, rank 18 that one in the best position.

[b] In some cases, the increase in debt and/or the change in debt-service ratios has to be calculated for shorter periods because of lacking data which may slightly distort the ranking with respect to these indicators.

Sources: Tables 10, 11, 13, 15; IMF, *International Financial Statistics.*

tries included, the debt situation was significantly less troublesome. It is striking that, with the exception of Korea, all Asian borrowers belonged to the last mentioned group. Sharply contrasting with this, only one country from Latin America (Colombia) was included here.

To be sure, some objections may be raised against the indicator approach. In the first instance it has to be admitted that a definition of critical indicator values is impossible. An individual borrower reaching or exceeding specific indicator levels does not automatically mean that repayment problems will certainly emerge (Dhonte, 1979, pp. 63–76). Historical evidence shows that countries defaulted at comparatively low indicator levels, whereas, simultaneously, other borrowers avoided default though characterised by significantly higher indicator values (see, for example, Finch, 1951; Avramovic, 1958). This is mainly due to the fact that the most frequently used indicators are not based on a productivity concept indicating the amount of foreign capital inflows which a borrower can take up with economic benefit (OECD, 1974; Sachs, 1982, p. 240–1). Hence the predictive value of indicator systems is limited, especially in the longer run. What is presented instead is a picture of the short-run rigidity in the borrowers' indebtedness and the pressure to which they are exposed in view of their present balance of payments and general domestic economic conditions.

It is in this latter respect that the conclusion may be drawn from the above analysis that most of the Latin American countries can be considered problem borrowers as defined earlier. The group of Asian economies was in a significantly better position.

The identification of problem countries may be further checked by analysing the credit rating of major borrowers in international capital markets. Table 17 refers to the system presented every six months by the Institutional Investor Magazine. The index defining '100' as an ideal position reflects the credit-worthiness of public debtors in about 100 countries. Although similar limitations will apply to rating systems as already discussed in connection with debt indicators (Sjaastad, 1983, p. 310), the classification may be crucial for many borrowers considering the very fact that

Table 17: Credit Rating of Major Third World Borrowing Countries, 1981–83

	March 1981		September 1981	March 1982	September 1982	March 1983	September 1983	
	Rating	Rank[a]	Rank[a]	Rank[a]	Rank[a]	Rank[a]	Rating	Rank[a]
Argentina	63.4	30	42	48	64	70	28.2	70
Brazil	49.8	54	50	49	42	42	37.6	51
Chile	54.4	47	46	44	44	47	32.8	62
Colombia	59.0	34	36	40	34	34	51.0	39
Egypt	36.0	71	67	69	65	64	33.5	61
India	49.9	53	52	52	48	45	46.2	43
Indonesia	57.1	41	38	35	35	37	51.6	37
Ivory Coast	44.3	61	63	64	61	59	35.3	58
Republic of Korea	55.4	46	39	34	32	32	56.4	31
Malaysia	72.8	22	19	19	20	19	69.1	20
Mexico	71.4	23	25	29	37	58	33.9	60
Nigeria	55.8	45	43	43	46	49	36.3	55
Philippines	44.3	61	54	62	59	62	32.6	63
Thailand	52.2	49	48	47	43	41	52.2	36
Turkey	13.7	92	91	85	78	75	26.0	73
Venezuela	69.3	28	29	28	29	30	43.4	45
Yugoslavia	50.4	52	54	61	60	66	29.9	66
Zaire	6.8	98	102	103	n.a.	n.a.	6.9	104

[a] Among the about 100 countries included in the rating system.

Source: Institutional Investor Magazine.

private lenders frequently rely on schemes of this sort. Accordingly, a country which is conceived as a problem borrower will sooner or later run into difficulties in obtaining fresh money. A realisation of the earlier mistrust will become highly probable in this way, particularly for those debtors which heavily depend on non-official capital inflows.

Table 17 offers quite interesting insights concerning developments in the credit rating of our sample countries in the recent past. In early 1981 the rating was relatively favourable for a rather heterogeneous set of borrowers. The rating exceeded 50 for major oil exporters—Indonesia, Mexico, Nigeria, Venezuela—for Asian (Korea, Malaysia, Thailand) as well as for Latin American non-oil economies (Argentina, Chile, Colombia) and for Yugoslavia. Yet, a rather firm correlation existed between a high credit rating and a relatively comfortable debt situation prevailing at the beginning of the eighties and vice versa (Table 18). A comparatively favourable rating went along with low shares of debt in GDP and exports and with only moderate increases in debt-service ratios. Additionally, some other economic characteristics of borrowing countries significantly influenced their credit-worthiness. Countries relatively well advanced in terms of GDP per capita and the industrialisation level reached were ranked higher than borrowers falling behind. On the other hand, both a high import share in domestic energy consumption and a large proportion of export earnings being absorbed by the oil-import bill contributed to a scaling down in terms of credit-worthiness.

Within two and a half years the credit rating for all sample countries deteriorated drastically from an average of 50.3 to 39.1. Parallel to this overall decline, there were heavy fluctuations with respect to the ranking. On the losers' side, Argentina must be mentioned in the first place, whose rank within the sample dropped from position four to sixteen. A similar worsening was experienced by Mexico, falling from position two to eleven. Of the three other countries for which a decline of four rank positions is reported, two were located in Latin America—Chile and Venezuela—the third being Yugoslavia. Among the remaining five borrowers whose rating still exceeded 50, Colombia stood alone from

Table 18: Rank Correlations between the Credit Rating of Major Third World Borrowing Countries in Early 1981 and Some Debt Indicators[a]

Debt indicators[b]			General economic indicators[c]	
Total debt	(1)	0.08	GDP per capita	0.51**
Total debt per capita	(2)	0.21	Growth of GDP per	
Total debt as percent of			capita	0.13
GDP	(3)	−0.59***	Net imports of	
Total debt as percent of			commercial energy	
merchandise exports	(4)	−0.52**	as percent of total	
Debt service as percent			consumption of	
of GDP	(5)	−0.23	commercial energy	−0.52**
Debt service as percent			Net oil imports as	
of merchandise ex-			percent of total	
ports	(6)	−0.35†	exports	−0.60***
Nominal annual aver-				
age			Industry as percent	
growth rate for total			of GDP	0.58**
debt, 1978–80	(7)	0.07	Exports as percent	
Real annual average			of GDP	0.10
growth rate for total			Manufactured ex-	
debt, 1978–80	(8)	−0.25	ports as percent of	
Increase in debt service			total exports	−0.26
as percent of GDP,				
1978–80	(9)	−0.53**		
Increase in debt service				
as percent of mer-				
chandise exports,				
1978–80	(10)	−0.43*		
Average position ac-				
cording to indicators				
(1)–(10)		−0.46*		
Average position ac-				
cording to indicators				
(3)–(6) and (8)–(10)		−0.66***		

[a] *** Indicates significance at the 1 percent level; ** 2.5 percent level; * 5 percent level; † 10 percent level.
[b] All indicators for 1980 if not otherwise stated.
[c] As defined in Table 10.

Sources: Tables 10, 11, 13, 15, 16; IMF, *International Financial Statistics*.

Latin America against four Asian countries—Malaysia, Korea, Thailand and Indonesia, in descending order of rank positions. In particular, Korea and Thailand jumped up by six and seven positions, respectively, ranked second and

Table 19: Debt Problems in Major Third World Borrowing Countries, 1981–83[a]

	Problems in servicing foreign debt: delays and arrears in transferring interest and amortisation payments	Moratoriums unilaterally declared or mutually agreed upon	Reschedulings arranged or asked for	Bridging finance obtained or asked for	Difficulties in raising new loans: reluctance of foreign banks to provide fresh money: interruptions in rolling-over debt
	(1)	(2)	(3)	(4)	(5)
Argentina	1982: 2 1983: 2	1982: 2[b] 1983: 2	1982/3: 2	1982: 1 1983: 1	1982: 2 1983: 2
Brazil	1982: 1 1983: 2	1982/3: 2	1982: 2 1983: 2	1982: 1 1983: 1	1982: 2 1983: 2
Chile	1983: 2	1983: 2	1983: 2	1982: 1 1983: 1	1982: 2 1983: 2
Colombia					1983: 1
Egypt	1983: 2	1983: 1[h]			
India					
Indonesia	1983: 1				1983: 1
Ivory Coast			1983: 2		1982: 2
Rep. of Korea	1981: 1				1982: 1 1983: 1
Malaysia					
Mexico	1982: 2 1983: 2	1982: 2 1983: 2	1982: 2 1983: 2	1982: 1 1983: 1	1981: 1 1982: 2
Nigeria	1982: 2 1983: 2		1983: 2		1982: 1 1983: 2
Philippines	1983: 2	1983: 2	1983: 2	1983: 1	1982: 1 1983: 2
Thailand					1983: 1
Turkey	1981: 2 1982: 1		1981: 2 1982: 2	1981: 1	1981: 2 1982: 1
Venezuela	1981: 1 1982: 2 1983: 2	1983: 2	1982: 2 1983: 2		1982: 2 1983: 2
Yugoslavia	1982: 2 1983: 2	1983: 2	1982: 1[c] 1983: 2	1982: 1 1983: 1	1981: 1 1982: 2 1983: 2
Zaire	1981: 2 1982: 2 1983: 2	1981: 2	1981: 2 1982: 2 1983: 2		

[a] In order to differentiate at least tentatively between different degrees of debt difficulties, weights are attached to each case. In case of only minor difficulties (for example: delays in debt-servicing being only short or being restricted to a negligible share of foreign loans; only a minority of lenders being reluctant to provide fresh money; private banks' concerns being limited to special aspects of the borrower's foreign indebtedness or being offset by a favourable perception of other banks; a less remarkable hardening in loan conditions; unconditional official stand-by credits) half the normal weight is given. The normal weight is '2' for events listed in columns (1)–(3), (5) and (6) which are most indicative of debt problems, and '1' for columns (4) and (7)–(9) which can be conceived as less important.

Table 19—continued

	Private banks' concern about the borrowing country's debt situation; private banks' demands for an IMF agreement	Significant hardening of loan conditions	Negotiations with IMF or similar international organisations on official credit programmes	Pressures by lenders' governments or international organisations on private banks to grant further loans	Sum of weights in (1)–(9)
	(6)	(7)	(8)	(9)	(10)
Argentina	1981: 2 1982: 2 1983: 2	1981/2: 1	1982: 1		24
Brazil	1982: 2 1983: 2	1981: 1	1982: 1 1983: 1	1982: 1 1983: 1	24
Chile	1983: 2	1981: 1 1983: 1	1982: 1 1983: 1	1983: 0.5[g]	18.5
Colombia		1983: 1			2
Egypt					3
India			1981: 1		1
Indonesia	1983: 1	1983: 1			4
Ivory Coast	1983: 1		1981: 1		6
Rep. of Korea	1981: 1 1983: 1	1982/3: 1	1981: 0.5 1983: 0.5		7
Malaysia		1982: 1 1983: 0.5			1.5
Mexico	1982: 2	1981: 0.5 1982: 1 1983: 1	1982/3: 1	1982: 1	23.5
Nigeria	1982: 2 1983: 2	1982: 1	1982: 0.5[d] 1983: 1		15.5
Philippines	1983: 2	1982: 0.5 1983: 1	1982: 0.5 1983: 1	1983: 1	16
Thailand					1
Turkey			1981: 1[e] 1983: 0.5	1981: 1	13.5
Venezuela	1981: 1 1983: 2	1981: 0.5 1982: 1	1983: 1[f]		20.5
Yugoslavia	1982: 2 1983: 2	1981: 0.5 1983: 0.5	1983: 1	1981/2: 1 1983: 1	24
Zaire			1981/2: 1 1983: 1		16

[b] Payments due to Great Britain blocked because of Falkland conflict. In addition, growing pressures on Argentina's government to declare a unilateral moratorium on all foreign debts.
[c] Discussed and demanded for by the Bank for International Settlements.
[d] Discussed only.
[e] Negotiations with the OECD.
[f] Adoption of a formal IMF economic stabilisation programme refused after internal discussions.
[g] Expected.
[h] Only with respect to USSR.

Source: Own compilation on the basis of various press reports.

third within the sample in September 1983. Korea alone was successful in improving its rating in absolute terms, disregarding the improvement of Turkey and Zaire, which took place at an extremely low rating level.

Hence, the perception of international capital markets regarding the borrowers' credit-worthiness strongly confirms the results shown by the indicator approach. The problem countries seemed to be mainly located in Latin America. In addition, for African borrowers like Zaire and, to a somewhat lesser extent, for Egypt and the Ivory Coast (both with a slight relative improvement in credit rating in the most recent past), as well as for European debtors, especially for Turkey, the debt situation proved to be rather difficult.[5] The bulk of Asian borrowers, however, could not be regarded as problem countries.

Table 19 gives some further insights with respect to different forms in which debt problems may emerge. The short review focuses on the following aspects, though there is, undoubtedly, considerable overlapping:

1. Problems in servicing foreign debt; delays and arrears in transferring interest and amortisation payments falling due.
2. Moratoriums unilaterally declared or mutually agreed upon.
3. Reschedulings of foreign debt arranged by negotiations with private and official creditors or asked for by borrowers.
4. Bridging finance obtained or asked for.
5. Difficulties in raising further loans; reluctance of foreign banks to provide fresh money: interruptions in the process of rolling-over foreign debt.
6. Private bankers' concern about the borrowers' debt situation; private creditors' demands for an IMF agreement as a prerequisite to a continued private credit engagement.
7. Hardening of loan conditions, especially spreads above LIBOR (London Interbank Offered Rate) and fees.
8. Negotiations with the IMF or other international organisations on official credit programmes.
9. Pressures by lenders' governments or international

organisations like the IMF on private banks to grant further loans ('involuntary' private lending).

The analysis which seeks to identify those sample countries faced with difficulties listed above concentrates on the early eighties because debt problems deteriorated considerably in this period. Moreover, possible worldwide financial drawbacks arising out of the Third World's international indebtedness (the topic of Ch. 9) will heavily depend on recent developments which, in many cases, cannot be considered as resolved as yet. The overview presented in Table 19 is based on a comprehensive review of press reports. This procedure has some shortcomings. Probably the press is primarily interested in the most important debtors, whereas the information base is rather weak in the case of some smaller countries which may be neglected by the press. In addition, the assessment of events is highly subjective, especially the evaluation of private bankers' concerns and of difficulties in raising fresh money.

Nevertheless, the information in Table 19 is very illuminating in so far as it strongly supports the results presented above. Comparing the sum of weights in column 10, a clear distinction can be drawn between a group of ten countries—Argentina, Brazil, Chile, Mexico, Nigeria, the Philippines, Turkey, Venezuela, Yugoslavia, Zaire—for which debt related difficulties proved to be most serious, and the rest of the sample. With the exception of Nigeria and the Philippines, this group fits the list of borrowers which were conceived as critical cases from different angles already. Thus it seems highly justified to call these eight countries the major problem borrowers within the sample. For Nigeria and the Philippines, debt problems reported in Table 19 were of a very recent nature; this is the reason why difficulties were not reflected in debt indicators before, which—due to the non-availability of data—could not be calculated for the most recent past.[6] Again in accordance with earlier impressions, in particular, Colombia, India, Indonesia, Malaysia and Thailand can be regarded as sound debtors. For them the sum of weights in column 10 is very low. For borrowers like Egypt, the Ivory Coast and Korea the picture is a little more ambiguous. In some respects their debt situation seemed more difficult to manage. Compared to the above-mentioned problem borrowers, however, foreign indebtedness proved to be far less troublesome for them.

NOTES

1. If short-term loans are accounted for, the computed debt burden increases considerably; *see* as a complement to Table 15 the estimated debt-service ratios for 1983 in Table 12. In cases where the roll-over of short-term credits was still smoothly functioning, amortisation of short-term loans however remained rather fictitious.
2. Regarding the change in debt-service ratios from 1978 to the early eighties (instead of the level of ratios in 1980), for three countries which experienced a sharp increase in indebtedness either the deterioration in DS/E and DS/GDP was only marginal (Philippines, DS/E; Thailand, DS/GDP; Mexico, DS/GDP) or the ratios even improved (Philippines, DS/GDP; Thailand, DS/E; Mexico, DS/E).
3. Ranked in descending order according to the method described above. The change in ratios DS/E and DS/GDP was calculated for the period 1978–82 for the former and 1978–81 for the latter; the year 1982 was left out of account in the case of DS/GDP because of availability of the required data for only seven countries. In some cases the change in DS/E and DS/GDP has to be calculated for shorter periods because of non-availability of data which may slightly distort the ranking.
4. For sure, the rank correlation approach has some shortcomings. The major weakness of this technique is that it does not allow for the distance between two rank positions. Thus, a very large difference between ranks 1 and 2, for example, has the same weight as a rather small margin between ranks 2 and 3. Regression analysis may be thought of as the principal alternative approach. In the present context of identifying the problem borrowers, however, this technique is not applicable.
5. Nigeria, as the fourth African country included, was in a quite favourable debt position for long. However, in the early eighties it experienced a significant deterioration.
6. This again hints at the inadequacy of using debt-service indicators etc. for predicting future difficulties in handling foreign debt.

5 External Shocks as Causes for Debt Problems

Turning to an analysis of underlying factors which may have caused the foreign debt situation of many Third World borrowers to deteriorate, the main responsibility is very often given to developments which are outside the control of the debtor countries. According to a widespread impression, it is in the non-oil developing countries in particular that economic prospects have been negatively affected by the severe external shocks in the seventies and early eighties. Many countries, confronted with a rather grim international economic environment, tried to circumvent an immediate and drastic cut in domestic absorption. An easy way to stretch the adjustment process was to enhance capital inflows at least temporarily, hoping for worldwide improvement in economic conditions. However, most of these hopes were belied. Before previous shocks had been overcome, the borrowers were hit by new ones, which sometimes seemed to result in even greater troubles for the Third World. As the intensified recourse to foreign capital was based on the now vanishing illusion of only short-term economic disturbances, the emergence of debt-servicing problems could no longer be avoided.

It is the major aim of this chapter to test this hypothesis. An attempt is made to quantify the impact that major external shocks have exerted since 1973 on the balance of payments position, both of NOPECs as a group and of eighteen sample countries individually, thereby indicating their (additional) needs in foreign capital. Taking 1973 as a starting point is by no means denying that external shocks had already occurred in the sixties and early seventies. However, those factors which are commonly understood as having been crucial in aggravating the Third World's debt situation will be captured by concentrating on 1973 onwards:

51

1. In 1973/74, OPEC was successful in dramatically raising the export price for oil, which on an average soared
   from $2 to $3 (US) per barrel to more than $11. The
   year 1979/80 saw the second oil-price shock, oil prices
   finally reaching a level of $32 to $40 per barrel.
   According to most observers, the balance of payments
   burden caused by OPEC's price policy was to be felt
   most heavily in developing countries dependent on oil
   imports. It was stressed that, in contrast to advanced
   industrial economies, developing countries could
   hardly save energy without affecting future growth and
   industrialisation prospects. Moreover, their ability to
   substitute oil with other energy sources was perceived
   to be comparatively limited.

2. Both the first oil-price shock and anti-inflationary fiscal
   and monetary policies in major industrial countries
   resulted in a severe international recession in the mid-
   seventies, which could have hampered the Third
   World's economic situation in two ways. The slackening world-market demand not only threatened a continuous growth in export volumes but was also likely to
   force export prices down. As the growth performance
   of most of the industrial countries remained gloomy
   throughout the seventies and early eighties, the loss in
   export earnings was probably further increased. This
   was all the more to be expected as protectionist
   measures imposed by major trading partners simultaneously gathered momentum.

3. A third factor which is often considered as being
   responsible for debt problems in the Third World is the
   sudden shift in monetary policies, especially in the
   United States. Monetary restrictions after 1980 led to a
   scarcity of US-dollar supplies and, consequently, to a
   further appreciation of this currency. This has two
   important consequences for the borrowers. First, due
   to the exchange-rate effect, the level of indebtedness
   already accumulated increased in terms of the borrower's own currency (i.e. the amount of domestic
   resources required to repay one US dollar increased).
   Second, interest rates in international capital markets

shot up and that increased the debt-service burden for both floating-interest loans raised in the past and all new credits.

Quantifying the impact of external shocks on the balance of payments and debt situation of borrowing economies requires some assumptions. In order to be able to differentiate world-market effects from influences arising out of the Third World's domestic policies, it has to be assumed that developing countries may be labelled as small economies in the sense that export and import prices are exogenously determinated by the overall world-market demand and supply. Their own market shares are regarded as too small to significantly affect world-market prices. This seems most realistic for imports of developing countries. On the export side, some qualifications may seem in place. Especially in the field of raw materials and agricultural products, world-market prices may be influenced by export variations of some major Third World suppliers. On an aggregate export level, however, this should be of only minor importance for the majority of developing countries; by and large, the price-taking assumption seems to hold for exports, too.

Both OPEC's oil-price policy and the retarding economic growth in industrial countries are supposed to cause the NOPECs' terms-of-trade to deteriorate. These effects will be accounted for by firstly calculating hypothetical export and import flows for all NOPECs and the eighteen sample countries for the period 1974–82 on the basis of unchanged prices of 1973. Afterwards, hypothetical trade figures will be deducted from exports and imports at current prices. Accordingly, the aggregated terms-of-trade effect on the balance of payments position (E_{tot}) can be written as:[1]

$$E_{tot} = \sum_{t=1974}^{1982} [Imv^t \cdot (p_{im}^t - p_{im}^{1973}) - Exv^t \cdot (p_{ex}^t - p_{ex}^{1973})]$$

where:

Imv, Exv = volumes of imports and exports
p_{im}, p_{ex} = prices of imports and exports.

It is to be expected that a large part of the just-defined

overall terms-of-trade induced additional financial needs was due to the dramatic rise in oil-import bills. To check this, the oil-price effects can be separated from the overall terms-of-trade impact. This was done for 1974–81 only, because import volumes of crude petroleum and petroleum products were not available later on. Similar to the above-described procedure, hypothetical net oil-import payments[2] were calculated by multiplying current net import volumes of crude petroleum and petroleum products with the average oil prices of 1971–73,[3] which then were confronted with actual payments of 1974–81.[4] Formally expressed, the aggregated oil-price effect (E_{oil}) amounts to:

$$E_{oil} = \sum_{t=1974}^{1981} [(PIm^t - PEx^t) - p_p^{71/3} \cdot (PImv^t - PExv^t)]$$

where:

PIm, PEx = current import and export values of crude petroleum and petroleum products

PImv, PExv = current import and export volumes of crude petroleum and petroleum products

$p_p^{71/3}$ = weighted average unit values of net imports or exports of crude petroleum and petroleum products for the base period of 1971–73.

In contrast to import and export prices which are assumed as being externally determined, trade volumes may be controlled by domestic policies pursued by the borrowing countries. The question of to which extent the Third World succeeded in reducing its foreign capital needs by restricting imports and by expanding exports will be raised in the next chapter. With respect to export volumes, however, there are both internal and external forces at work. An important external factor not only influencing export prices but also affecting real world-market sales is commonly seen in the weak growth performance of industrial countries, the impact of which, presumably, was further aggravated by an intensi-fied recourse to protectionist measures by the Third World's major trading partners.

In order to separate external from internal effects on the

export side, the procedure is as follows.[5] Hypothetical export volumes for the years 1974–82 are introduced on the assumption that the exporting country maintained its share in world export-markets, as in the base period of 1970–73. The difference between actual and hypothetical exports will be attributed to domestic policy actions later on. The effects of changes in world-market demand are accounted for by, first, estimating trend exports for the country under consideration on the assumption that in 1974–82 world-trade volumes developed as in the sixties and early seventies and that the country's export-market share remained unchanged.[6] Second, trend figures are compared to hypothetical exports. Consequently, the aggregated export short-fall due to a (relative) reduction in real world-market demand (E_{wmd}) may be written as:[7]

$$E_{wmd} = \sum_{t=1974}^{1982} (Exv_{tr}^t - Exv_{hyp}^t)$$

$$= \sum_{t=1974}^{1982} [MS^{70/3} \cdot (WExv_{tr}^t - WExv_{act}^t)]$$

where:

Exv_{tr}, Exv_{hyp} = trend and hypothetical export volumes of the country under consideration

$MS^{70/3}$ = export share in world markets of the country under consideration in the base period of 1970–73

$WExv_{tr}$, WEx-
v_{act} = trend and actual export volumes of all world-market suppliers.

Finally, the balance of payments effects of rising interest rates on foreign loans are quantified. Again the early seventies act as a base period: interest rates of 1972/73 are compared with rates prevailing later on. Hypothetical interest payments for 1974–83 are calculated by assuming constant 1972/73 interest rates throughout the whole period under consideration and by multiplying these rates with total debt outstanding in the years 1973–82.[8] By multiplying interest-rate differentials with total debt outstanding one comes up with the additional debt-service burden due to rising interest rates (E_{ir}):

$$E_{ir} = \sum_{t=1974}^{1983} [(i^t - i^{72/3}) \cdot D^{t-1}]$$

where:

i^t, $i^{72/3}$ = current interest rates and interest rates for the
base period 1972/73

D = total debt outstanding.

Because of some data shortcomings, this procedure only allows an approximation of interest-rate-induced additional capital requirements. As already mentioned in Chapter 3, debt figures disregard short-term loans, with the exception of data for all NOPECs. Consequently, interest-rate effects will be understated for individual sample countries, since the seventies and eighties experienced a rising share of short-term debt. For countries temporarily reporting public and publicly guaranteed debt only, the understatement may be further enlarged. However, since data on non-guaranteed private debt were predominantly missing for the first half of the seventies only, the effect in question may be largely offset by a compensating influence: for thirteen out of eighteen sample countries, average interest rates in 1972/73 have to be calculated on the basis of public and publicly guaranteed debt.[9] Since comparatively high interest rates are typically levied on non-guaranteed credits, reference interest rates of 1972/73 will be biased on the lower side, which results in an overstatement of interest-rate differentials and additional interest-payment burdens. Hence, overall distortions may be supposed as playing an only minor role.

The calculations just described are presented in Tables 20 to 24. Besides shedding some light on the overall importance of different external shocks in explaining the NOPECs' foreign debt situation, we will concentrate on differences between individual borrowers by asking to which extent their international indebtedness could have been due to negative external effects. This is not to say that in the absence of external shocks their debt accumulated in the

Table 20: Terms-of-Trade Effects on the Balance of Payments Position of Major Third World Borrowing Countries, 1974–82[a] (in billions of US$)

	1974	1975	1976	1977	1978	1979	1980	1981	1982	Σ 1974–82[b]	Import price effects Σ 1974–82[b]	Export price effects Σ 1974–82[b]
All NOPECs	18.2	34.5	25.2	20.1	35.4	45.8	77.2	100.2	n.a.	356.6	1086.9	730.3
Argentina	0.3	1.1	1.1	1.7	1.6	2.0	4.1	3.3	n.a.	15.2	22.9	7.7
Brazil	2.8	3.3	2.2	0.2	1.9	4.0	6.5	6.0	5.8	32.6	84.1	51.5
Chile	0.2	0.7	0.7	1.2	1.6	1.7	2.3	4.0	n.a.	12.4	15.0	2.6
Colombia	-0.0	0.8	-0.3	-0.9	-0.6	-0.4	-0.0	1.1	1.3	0.2	12.9	12.7
Egypt	0.1	0.8	0.8	1.3	2.5	1.2	1.2	3.6	n.a.	11.6	19.9	8.3
India	1.2	2.1	1.4	0.7	1.2	2.5	5.5	n.a.	n.a.	14.5	29.0	14.5
Indonesia	-3.2	-2.7	-3.4	-4.7	-4.6	-7.9	-11.7	-10.6	n.a.	-48.8	26.5	75.3
Ivory Coast	-0.1	0.0	-0.2	-0.6	-0.4	-0.2	-0.1	0.2	n.a.	-1.3	7.8	9.1
Rep. of Korea	1.5	2.0	1.4	1.0	1.4	3.3	5.1	5.8	4.0	25.5	74.2	48.7
Malaysia	-0.2	0.2	-0.6	-0.9	-1.0	-3.0	-2.5	-0.6	0.1	-8.4	32.1	40.5
Mexico	0.7	1.1	0.9	0.6	1.1	2.4	2.9	4.4	n.a.	14.2	41.4	27.1
Nigeria	-5.7	-3.5	-4.7	-4.8	-2.2	-9.1	-14.2	-6.0	n.a.	-50.3	39.5	89.8
Philippines	0.3	1.0	1.3	1.5	1.6	1.9	3.0	3.5	4.0	18.0	29.0	10.9
Thailand	0.5	1.0	1.1	1.6	1.8	2.2	3.1	3.8	3.5	18.5	33.6	15.1
Turkey	0.8	1.6	1.6	2.2	1.6	2.0	4.1	4.3	3.8	22.0	32.1	10.1
Venezuela	-5.6	-3.4	-3.0	-1.5	-0.5	-4.4	-7.9	-7.9	n.a.	-34.0	44.8	78.8
Yugoslavia	1.6	1.6	1.2	2.3	2.2	3.7	4.1	n.a.	n.a.	16.6	33.7	17.1
Zaire	-0.0	0.4	0.2	0.1	0.2	-0.1	-0.0	0.3	n.a.	1.0	2.6	1.6

[a] For method of calculation, see the text. A negative sign denotes a terms-of-trade improvement i.e. a balance of payments alleviation.
[b] For some countries, totals are for 1974–81 or 1974–80 only. Slight discrepancies are due to rounding.

Sources: IMF, *International Financial Statistics*; UNCTAD, *Handbook of International Trade and Development Statistics.*

past would have been reduced accordingly, that is, by the same amount as indicated as balance of payments impact of world-market developments in Tables 20 to 24. To borrow in excess of the originally planned foreign capital inflows was only one mode of adjustment to external shocks. A foreign exchange gap could be narrowed in other ways, especially by curtailing imports and stimulating exports, which is one of the subjects of the next chapter. What can be compared, however, is the degree of adjustment required by unfavourable impacts from outside and the severity of problems potentially arising out of external shocks. In particular, the hypothesis that a strong relationship prevails between the balance of payments effects of world-market factors and the emergence of debt crises (i.e. the perception that especially countries that suffered most from external shocks will run into debt difficulties) can be checked.

For the NOPECs as a group, the terms-of-trade effect clearly dominated both the real world-market-demand effect and the interest-rate effect. Losses for the period 1974–81 reached $357 billion (Table 20); that is, 79 per cent of long-term debt in 1981 or 9.5 per cent of the NOPECs' total nominal external trade flows in 1974–81. They culminated in the last two years under consideration when import prices shot up by 25 per cent, whereas export prices rose by only 9 per cent.

For major individual borrowers, however, the role of terms-of-trade developments differed sharply. As could be expected, OPEC members Venezuela, Indonesia and Nigeria derived great advantage from soaring oil prices. For them export-price improvements outpaced the rise in import prices, resulting in net additional world-market earnings of between $34 billion and $50 billion. Table 10 underlines the decisive role of oil exports, especially in Nigeria and Venezuela. Additionally, Malaysia as another net oil exporter benefited from terms-of-trade gains in 1974–81. The same accrued to Colombia and the Ivory Coast, both characterised by small net oil-import bills relative to total exports (see Table 10) and where, consequently, the balance of payments was only marginally affected by oil-price-induced additional oil-import payments.[10]

On the other hand, the rather favourable energy position of Egypt, Mexico and, to a lesser extent, Argentina and Zaire did not prevent them from being confronted with deteriorating terms-of-trade. Relative to outstanding debt and external trade, losses remained comparatively small for Zaire (25 per cent and 6.9 per cent, respectively) and Mexico (27 per cent and 9.4 per cent). They were significantly higher for Egypt (77 per cent and 21.2 per cent) and Argentina (64 per cent and 16.3 per cent), the latter country suffering from an extremely unfavourable development in export prices.

Quite interesting are differences between those sample countries heavily depending on energy imports. For this subgroup, oil-price-induced additional import payments contributed considerably to the overall balance of payments burden resulting from rising import prices; with the exception of Yugoslavia, where the oil-price factor accounted for 22 per cent of total additional import payments, a third to slightly more than a half of overall import price effects were due to OPEC's price policy (Table 21). Most remarkably, the *relative* balance of payments effect of deteriorating terms-of-trade was comparatively modest in the case of Brazil, although, in *absolute* terms, its losses were the highest of all borrowers under consideration. In 1974–81 they amounted to 41 per cent of long-term debt outstanding in 1981 and 10.8 per cent of total exports and imports in 1974–81. This contrasted sharply with Asian countries like Thailand and the Philippines, where the respective figures stood at 205 per cent and 140 per cent (relative to long-term debt) and 18.7 per cent and 18.9 per cent (relative to external trade), the remaining borrowers lying in between with only two exceptions.[11]

Summing up, it is striking that the results of Table 20 do not point to a strong correlation between the balance of payments impact of negative external shocks in the form of terms-of-trade losses and the emergence of debt problems. On the contrary, for some of those countries most severely hit by worsening terms-of-trade, the external debt situation did not cause major troubles; this was particularly to be observed in Asia. On the other hand, for Latin American

Table 21: Oil-Price Effects on the Balance of Payments Position of Major Third World Borrowing Countries, 1974–81

	Oil-price-induced additional oil import payments[a]		
	in billions of US$	as percent of terms-of-trade effects[b]	as percent of import price effects[b,c]
Argentina	2.47	16.3	10.8
Brazil	38.27	142.8	54.6
Chile	n.a.	n.a.	n.a.
Colombia	0.62[d]	n.a.[e]	8.8[d]
Egypt	n.a.	n.a.	n.a.
India	14.10[d]	97.2[d]	48.5[d]
Indonesia	−51.96	106.5	69.0
Ivory Coast	1.07	n.a.[e]	13.6
Republic of Korea	21.31	99.1	35.8

	Oil-price-induced additional oil import payments[a]		
	in billions of US$	as percent of terms-of-trade effects[b]	as percent of import price effects[b,c]
Malaysia	n.a.	n.a.	n.a.
Mexico	−25.39	n.a.[f]	93.6
Nigeria	−87.56	174.1	97.5
Philippines	8.94	63.9	37.8
Thailand	9.97	66.5	36.2
Turkey	12.25	67.3	47.7
Venezuela	−77.09	226.7	97.9
Yugoslavia	7.51[d]	45.2[d]	22.3[d]
Zaire	n.a.	n.a.	n.a.

[a] For method of calculation, see the text. Oil imports (crude petroleum plus petroleum products) are on a net basis i.e. oil exports are deducted. Consequently, negative values for net oil exporters indicate oil-price-induced additional export proceeds.

[b] Due to data limitations oil-price effects could be calculated for 1974–81 only. Accordingly, oil-price effects are set relative to terms-of-trade effects and import-price effects of 1974–81.

[c] For net oil exporters: relative to export-price effects in 1974–81.

[d] 1974–80.

[e] Negative-signed terms-of-trade effect in 1974–80 (Colombia) and 1974–81 (Ivory Coast).

[f] Positive-signed terms-of-trade effect in 1974–81.

Sources: UN, *Yearbook of International Trade Statistics;* UN, *Yearbook of World Energy Statistics;* IMF, *International Financial Statistics.*

and African countries which proved to be problem borrowers, the terms-of-trade effects remained comparatively
weak or even positive. The most spectacular example in this
respect was Mexico. One may further add Brazil, Venezuela, the Ivory Coast, Nigeria and Zaire.

Turning to the effects of real world-market demand on the
developing countries' balance of payments position, the
most important findings presented in Table 22 may be
summarised as follows. The calculation for all NOPECs
resulted in a loss in exports of about $104 billion in the
period 1974–82, which was less than a third of the terms-of-
trade effects in the period 1974–81. Even if trend exports
were estimated according to the logarithmic trend equation
of world exports (i.e. referring to the upper extreme; see
n. 6), which would roughly double the impact of the relative
decline in world-market demand, real demand effects would
still be clearly dominated by external price shocks. Similar to
the terms-of-trade development, losses caused by reduced
real export sales were concentrated in the early eighties,
when growth rates in the industrial countries' GDP at
constant prices dwindled from an average of 4 per cent in the
second half of the seventies to less than 1 per cent.

The degree to which individual borrowers were hit by the
reduction in world-market demand depended on the export-
market shares they had reached in the base period of 1970–
73. Shares ranged from very low figures for the Ivory Coast,
Turkey, Zaire, Colombia and Egypt (from 0.14 to 0.23 per
cent in ascending order) to about 1.1 per cent for Venezuela
and Brazil. Consequently, the balance of payments impact
was highest in the latter two countries, followed by six more
borrowers suffering losses of more than $3 billion. Again,
the group of countries most severely hit by external shocks
consisted of both debtors which could be regarded as
problem borrowers—the most important being Brazil,
Argentina, Venezuela and Yugoslavia—and economies
such as Malaysia and Indonesia, for which debt problems
were largely unknown. On the other hand, a critical debt
situation emerged also in some of those countries which, at
least in absolute terms, were only slightly affected by the
slackening world-market demand (e.g. Chile, Egypt, the

Table 22: Real World-Market Demand Effects on the Balance of Payments Position of Major Third World Borrowing Countries, 1974–82[a] (in billions of US$)

	1974	1975	1976	1977	1978	1979	1980	1981	1982	Σ 1974–82
All NOPECs	-4.69	6.99	3.54	6.18	8.83	8.30	13.69	23.57	38.01	104.41
Argentina	-0.18	0.27	0.14	0.24	0.34	0.32	0.52	0.90	1.45	4.00
Brazil	-0.31	0.46	0.23	0.41	0.58	0.54	0.90	1.55	2.49	6.85
Chile	-0.09	0.13	0.07	0.11	0.16	0.15	0.25	0.43	0.70	1.92
Colombia	-0.06	0.10	0.05	0.09	0.12	0.11	0.19	0.32	0.52	1.44
Egypt	-0.07	0.10	0.05	0.09	0.12	0.12	0.19	0.33	0.53	1.46
India	-0.17	0.26	0.13	0.23	0.32	0.30	0.50	0.86	1.39	3.81
Indonesia	-0.15	0.22	0.11	0.20	0.28	0.26	0.43	0.75	1.21	3.32
Ivory Coast	-0.04	0.06	0.03	0.05	0.08	0.07	0.12	0.20	0.33	0.90
Rep. of Korea	-0.11	0.17	0.09	0.15	0.21	0.20	0.33	0.57	0.92	2.53
Malaysia	-0.16	0.24	0.12	0.21	0.30	0.28	0.46	0.80	1.29	3.54
Mexico	-0.13	0.19	0.10	0.17	0.24	0.23	0.38	0.65	1.05	2.89
Nigeria	-0.18	0.28	0.14	0.24	0.35	0.33	0.54	0.93	1.50	4.11
Philippines	-0.10	0.14	0.07	0.13	0.18	0.17	0.28	0.49	0.78	2.15
Thailand	-0.09	0.13	0.07	0.11	0.16	0.15	0.25	0.44	0.71	1.94
Turkey	-0.06	0.09	0.05	0.08	0.12	0.11	0.18	0.31	0.50	1.38
Venezuela	-0.30	0.44	0.22	0.39	0.56	0.53	0.87	1.49	2.41	6.61
Yugoslavia	-0.15	0.23	0.12	0.20	0.29	0.27	0.45	0.78	1.25	3.44
Zaire	-0.06	0.09	0.05	0.08	0.12	0.11	0.18	0.31	0.51	1.39

[a] For method of calculation, see the text. A negative sign denotes a favourable world-market-demand effect, i.e. a balance of payments alleviation.

Sources: IMF, *International Financial Statistics;* UNCTAD, *Handbook of International Trade and Development Statistics.*

Ivory Coast, Zaire and Turkey). Hence, the results of Table 22 are also in conflict with the hypothesis that emphasises the decisive role of external shocks in explaining difficulties in servicing foreign debt.

The quantitative impact of rising international interest rates on the balance of payments position of all NOPECs was comparable to real export-demand effects (Table 23). Interest-rate effects remained negligible up to 1977. They gained greater importance at the end of the seventies and jumped to between $20 billion and $32 billion annually from 1980 onwards.[12] Averaging 10.4 per cent in the early eighties, interest rates paid by NOPECs were about twice as high as in the base period. The additional interest burden of 1974–83 amounted to nearly 80 per cent of hypothetical interest payments, which were calculated on the assumption of interest rates of 1972/73 remaining constant.

Regarding interest-rate effects in absolute terms, by far the highest impact is reported for Brazil and Mexico ($20.5 billion and $11.3 billion), although for them interest rates were already high in 1972/73 (Brazil, 6.2 per cent; Mexico, 8.2 per cent); in the recent past, interest rates temporarily above 14 per cent were levied on Brazil and Mexico, as was the case for some other Latin American borrowers too. Next ranked Chile and Indonesia, with a little less than $6 billion each. For both countries, however, estimates may be biased on the higher side, considering the extraordinarily low reference measure. Probably, 1972/73 interest rates of only 1.3 per cent calculated for Chile and Indonesia were largely caused by peculiarities prevailing in the base period. As a consequence of multilateral debt-relief operations in 1970 (Indonesia) and 1972 (Chile) (OECD, 1982, Table 19) interest payments originally falling due in 1972/73 may be substantially lowered by postponing them to later periods. In five more sample countries interest-rate effects exceeded $2 billion in 1974–83 that is in Venezuela, Argentina, Yugoslavia, Turkey and Korea (in descending order of additional interest payments).

With the exceptions of Indonesia and Korea, all these countries could be classified as problem borrowers, which, in contrast to the findings discussed earlier, may back the

Table 23: Interest-Rate Effects on the Balance of Payments Position of Major Third World Borrowing Countries, 1974–83[a] (in billions of US$)

	Interest-rate effects										Σ 1974–83	Hypothetical interest payments at constant 1972/73 interest rates in 1974–83[b]	Total interest-rate effects as percent of hypothetical interest payments
	1974	1975	1976	1977	1978	1979	1980	1981	1982	1983			
All NOPECs	2.73	2.41	1.34	2.28	5.57	11.10	20.64	31.28	31.64	24.50	133.49	168.14	79.4
Argentina	0.02	0.01	0.03	-0.01	0.14	0.04	0.30	0.54	1.52	0.95	3.54	8.80	40.2
Brazil	0.68	0.86	0.27	0.24	0.90	1.81	2.84	4.05	5.11	3.70	20.46	25.13	81.4
Chile	0.05	0.12	0.16	0.17	0.30	0.48	0.71	1.00	1.55	1.42	5.96	0.87	685.1
Colombia	0.02	0.01	0.02	0.02	0.05	0.12	0.11	0.34	n.a.	0.69	0.69	1.23	56.1
Egypt	0.01	0.04	-0.02	0.19	0.18	-0.02	-0.01	0.23	0.21	0.25	1.06	2.42	43.8
India	-0.01	-0.05	-0.05	-0.05	-0.03	-0.02	-0.13	-0.07	0.11	0.17	-0.15	3.98	-3.8
Indonesia	0.01	0.10	0.24	0.33	0.38	0.67	0.80	0.98	1.07	1.13	5.71	1.65	346.1
Ivory Coast	0.00	0.01	0.01	0.03	0.05	0.06	0.07	0.15	n.a.	n.a.	0.38	1.05	36.2
Rep. of Korea	-0.05	-0.02	0.00	-0.01	0.06	0.10	0.29	0.55	0.71	0.44	2.07	8.41	24.6
Malaysia	0.01	0.01	0.05	0.04	0.03	0.03	0.05	0.10	n.a.	n.a.	0.32	1.13	28.3
Mexico	0.12	0.15	0.20	0.00	0.16	0.94	1.92	2.74	1.71	3.33	11.27	25.11	44.9
Nigeria	-0.02	-0.02	-0.01	0.01	0.01	0.08	0.30	0.35	0.62	0.53	1.85	1.55	119.4
Philippines	0.01	0.00	0.02	0.02	0.05	0.16	0.21	0.26	0.48	0.46	1.67	3.13	53.4
Thailand	0.03	0.03	0.02	0.03	0.08	0.16	0.26	0.35	n.a.	0.64	0.96	1.16	82.8
Turkey	0.01	0.02	0.07	0.07	0.04	0.04	0.22	0.26	0.75	n.a.	2.12	2.56	82.8
Venezuela	0.02	0.02	0.06	0.03	0.13	0.26	0.66	1.06	1.19	0.87	4.30	5.64	76.2
Yugoslavia	0.00	0.01	-0.02	-0.04	0.08	0.20	0.45	0.76	0.65	0.51	2.60	5.63	46.2
Zaire	0.01	-0.01	-0.05	-0.05	-0.06	-0.10	-0.04	-0.09	n.a.	n.a.	-0.39	1.15	-33.9

[a] For method of calculation, see the text. If current interest rates are lower than in the base period of 1972/73, the calculation results in negative values i.e. a balance of payments alleviation.

[b] For some countries, totals are for 1974–82 or 1974–81 only. Slight discrepancies are due to rounding.

Sources: OECD, *Debt Problems of Developing Countries*; IMF,

widespread impression of a strong relationship between the balance of payments effects of external shocks and the existence of debt problems. Several points, however, may be raised against this conclusion. First of all, it has to be kept in mind that, compared to the terms-of-trade effects, external shocks in the form of rising interest rates were of only secondary importance. Regarding the nine countries listed above, losses due to deteriorating terms-of-trade clearly outpaced additional interest payments, apart from Indonesia and Venezuela, which both benefited from improved terms-of-trade. Second, problem borrowers are also to be found among those countries for which negligible interest-rate effects are presented in Table 23; mention may be made of Zaire, in particular.

Finally, it does not make much sense to focus exclusively on additional interest payments in absolute terms which not only depended on interest-rate developments but also on the amount of foreign debt accumulated. In order to isolate the external interest-rate factor, additional interest payments are expressed as a percentage of hypothetical interest payments calculated at constant 1972/73 interest rates (Table 23). In this relative perspective, only Brazil, Turkey and Venezuela remained in the top group, disregarding Chile and Indonesia for the above-mentioned reasons. Other countries where total interest-rate effects exceeded 50 per cent of hypothetical figures were Nigeria, Thailand, Colombia and the Philippines, two of which (Thailand and Colombia) had no major debt problems.

Adding up the balance of payments effects of major external shocks from 1974 onwards—that is the effects of changes in terms-of-trade, real world-market demand and international interest rates (Table 24)—some more generalised conclusions may be drawn. It has to be acknowledged that for the NOPECs as a group, unfavourable influences from outside caused severe adjustment problems. The aggregated impact of negative external shocks in 1974–81 exceeded long-term debt outstanding at the end of 1981. Nevertheless, results of this chapter are largely in conflict with the conventional wisdom of external shocks playing a decisive role in explaining the emergence of debt problems.

Table 24: Combined Effects of External Shocks on the Balance of Payments Position of Major Third World Borrowing Countries, 1974–82ᵃ (in billions of US$)

	1974	1975	1976	1977	1978	1979	1980	1981	1982	Σ 1974–82ᵇ	Impact of external shocks in 1974–81 as percent of debt in 1981ᶜ
All NOPECs	16.2	43.9	30.1	28.6	49.8	65.2	111.5	155.1	n.a.	570.0	110.5
Argentina	0.1	1.4	1.3	1.9	2.1	2.4	4.9	4.7	n.a.	21.8	79.5
Brazil	3.2	4.6	2.7	0.9	3.4	6.4	10.2	11.6	13.4	56.2	66.2
Chile	0.2	1.0	0.9	1.5	2.1	2.3	3.3	5.4	n.a.	18.9	139.9
Colombia	-0.0	0.1	-0.2	-0.8	-0.4	-0.2	0.3	1.8	n.a.	2.3	8.0
Egypt	0.0	0.9	0.8	1.6	2.8	1.3	1.4	4.2	n.a.	13.9	87.7
India	1.0	2.3	1.5	0.9	1.5	2.8	5.9	n.a.	n.a.	18.0	87.2ᵈ
Indonesia	-3.3	-2.4	-3.1	-4.2	-3.9	-7.0	-10.5	-8.9	n.a.	-40.9	-249.6
Ivory Coast	-0.1	0.1	-0.2	-0.5	-0.3	-0.1	0.1	0.4	n.a.	-0.0	-7.3
Rep. of Korea	1.3	2.2	1.5	1.1	1.7	3.6	5.7	6.9	5.6	29.7	122.8
Malaysia	-0.4	0.5	-0.4	-0.7	-0.7	-2.7	-2.0	0.3	n.a.	-4.5	-128.0
Mexico	0.7	1.4	1.2	0.8	1.5	3.6	5.2	7.8	n.a.	25.0	41.8
Nigeria	-5.9	-3.2	-4.6	-4.5	-1.8	-8.7	-13.4	-4.7	n.a.	-44.9	-783.7
Philippines	0.2	1.1	1.4	1.7	1.8	2.2	3.5	4.3	5.3	21.4	161.4
Thailand	0.4	1.2	1.2	1.7	2.0	2.5	3.6	4.6	n.a.	21.4	235.5
Turkey	0.7	1.7	1.7	2.4	1.8	2.2	4.5	4.9	5.1	24.9	136.9
Venezuela	-5.9	-2.9	-2.7	-1.1	0.2	-3.6	-6.4	-5.4	n.a.	-24.0	-185.2
Yugoslavia	1.4	1.8	1.3	2.5	2.6	4.2	5.0	n.a.	n.a.	22.1	123.6ᵈ
Zaire	-0.1	0.5	0.2	0.1	0.3	-0.1	0.1	0.5	n.a.	2.0	37.3

ᵃ Aggregation of terms-of-trade effects, real world-market-demand effects and interest-rate effects. A negative sign indicates positive external shocks i.e. a balance of payments alleviation.

ᵇ For shorter periods sometimes. In cases where, for example, the terms-of-trade effect could not be calculated whereas for the other two external effects figures are available these latter effects are accounted for in the sum for 1974–82, although a n.a. stands for the respective year.

ᶜ For means of comparison, the impact of external shocks in 1974–81 is set relative to (long-term) debt in 1981, instead of using 1974–82 and 1982 figures which are completely available for a few countries only. This restriction results in only minor discrepancies.

ᵈ External shocks in 1974–80 as percent of (long-term) debt in 1980.

According to Table 24 five countries were not hit at all. For them world-market developments rather resulted in a balance of payments alleviation, in most cases net oil exporters deriving advantage from rising oil prices. This did not prevent some of them, however, from running into debt-servicing difficulties, an outcome which sharply contradicts the hypothesis.

For those borrowers negatively affected, the balance of payments burden arising from external shocks was highly concentrated at the end of the period under consideration. In nine out of thirteen cases, more than two-thirds of the aggregated losses due to exogenous factors occurred from 1979 onwards. Although it is true that debt problems also gathered considerable momentum in the recent past only, it has to be considered that the enormous increase in foreign indebtedness was not restricted to the late seventies and early eighties and that, at least in some cases, difficulties in handling debt may be traced back to earlier times when external shocks were of minor importance.

Moreover, the group of countries which suffered most from unfavourable world-market conditions was not identical with the set of borrowers experiencing debt problems. In relative terms (i.e. as a percentage of debt outstanding) the impact of external shocks on the balance of payments in 1974–81 was strongest in Thailand, the Philippines, Chile, Turkey, Yugoslavia and Korea (in descending order). Notwithstanding, Korea and particularly Thailand proved to be rather sound debtors. On the other hand, for two of the three countries where the effects of external shocks amounted to less than 50 per cent of debt outstanding (i.e. Mexico and Zaire), major difficulties in servicing foreign loans were reported. Comparing Asian and Latin American sample countries, the following picture emerges. For debt-problem ridden Latin America, external shocks, on an average, accounted for 25 per cent of debt outstanding, whereas in Asia a far less troublesome debt situation went hand in hand with a significantly higher share of external shocks in foreign debt (38 per cent).[13] Accordingly, the deteriorating debt situation of many developing countries cannot be explained by exclusively referring to unfavourable developments outside the control of borrowers. At the very least, this hypothesis has to be supplemented. This is the topic of the next chapter, where the role of domestic policies with respect to the foreign debt situation is discussed.

NOTES

1. The first part of the expression shows the aggregated import-price effect, and the second part indicates the aggregated export-price effect on the balance of payments.
2. For major oil exporters included in the sample, the calculation results in hypothetical net earnings from oil exports.
3. As proxies for oil prices paid or received by individual sample countries, the weighted average unit values of net imports or exports of crude petroleum and petroleum products were taken. Against uniformly applying average world-market prices for oil for all sample countries, this procedure has the advantage of accounting for the considerable differences in oil prices between individual oil importers and exporters. On the importers' side, differences were probably mainly due to the specific structure of crude and processed oil imports and variations in sources from which oil imports originated. Averaging 1971–73 oil prices is for ruling out peculiarities of a single year, which otherwise may distort the reference price.
4. In some cases, actual net import payments or net export proceeds had to be estimated on the basis of incomplete data for 1980 and 1981. For some other countries the whole calculation proved impossible. Moreover, it has to be conceded that the calculation of oil-price effects may be slightly distorted by shifts in the oil-import structure after 1973, in regional terms as well as in terms of product structure. A stronger orientation of oil importers towards cheaper oil producers, for example, causes an understatement of the balance of payments impact of OPEC price policies.
5. This procedure was applied for the first time by Balassa. For a detailed description of the approach, *see*, for example, Balassa, 1981a; for further applications, *see* Balassa, 1981b; Agarwal, Glismann, Nunnenkamp, 1983; Nunnenkamp, 1979.
6. Both a linear and a logarithmic trend equation have been estimated for total exports of all world-market suppliers on the basis of figures for 1962–73. Both equations were statistically highly significant. They resulted, however, in marked differences in terms of predicted export figures for 1974–82. Whereas for the linear equation, trend figures exceeded actual world exports in only three years (1975, 1981, 1982), the logarithmic estimate showed a shortfall in world-trade volumes relative to trend figures from 1975 onwards. In order to rule out the

extremes, an average of both estimates was taken as a basis for calculating predicted trend figures for 1974–82. This resulted in an aggregated relative loss in real world-market sales of $625 billion or 10.7 per cent of actual trade volume in 1974–82.

7. In case of actual trade volume exceeding trend figures (i.e. a relative improvement of world-market-demand conditions), E_{wmd} will be negative-signed.

8. Calculating interest rates, annual interest payments were divided by debt outstanding at the end of the preceding year.

9. For the remaining five countries and for all NOPECs, interest rates of 1972/73 were calculated as weighted averages of interest rates for public and publicly guaranteed debt and rates for non-guaranteed private debt.

10. Moreover, export prices were well above the NOPEC average throughout the second half of the seventies and the early eighties for both Colombia and the Ivory Coast, which was largely due to sharply rising coffee and cocoa prices.

11. Relative to aggregated exports and imports in 1974–81, terms-of-trade losses exceeded the above-mentioned shares for Thailand and the Philippines in Turkey (28.2 per cent) and Chile (25.5 per cent).

12. For further coverage of this point, *see* Hope, 1981.

13. The difference in the importance of external shocks is further enlarged if countries are disregarded where exogenous factors resulted in a balance of payments alleviation (Venezuela in Latin America, Indonesia and Malaysia in Asia). After this adjustment one comes up with shares of 67 per cent in Latin America and 152 per cent in Asia.

6   Relevance of Domestic Policies in Borrowing Countries

According to the hypothesis raised in this chapter, developing countries have had quite a few instruments at their disposal to prevent the foreign debt situation from deteriorating. In the first instance, one may think of measures which may help adjustment to external shocks in a rather direct way. In order to restrict borrowing from abroad, an equilibrium in the trade balance may be restored by cutting imports or by implementing export promotion programmes. It is the first aim of this chapter to identify those borrowers who were successful in limiting external financing requirements in this way. There is an important difference between both strategies, however: only export promotion is well suited to help in the longer run, whereas a short-term success via import restrictions is likely to cause further adjustment problems later on, since significant import reductions will probably impede economic growth and export expansion. The range of governments' tools for preventing debt-servicing problems is however much wider. It is supposed that only if governments fail in bringing about adequate economic conditions (e.g. with respect to fiscal and monetary policies, industrialisation policies and exchange rate policy), foreign indebtedness is likely to pose major difficulties. That is why the following analysis should help to advise about domestic policies conceived as best suited to counter debt problems.

Turning to adjustments in the field of external trade first, assumptions made in the preceding chapter have to be recalled. Whereas import and export prices were exogenously given by world-market developments, trade volumes may be influenced by domestic policy actions. Especially on the import side, trade volumes will probably promptly react to governmental interferences. These may take two different

70

forms. The government may suppress domestic economic activity levels through restrictive fiscal and monetary policies which, as a corollary, will reduce import demand, with the import/GDP ratio remaining constant. On the other hand, import ratios may be squeezed (e.g. via protectionist measures). In the following, the former effect will be ignored, which seems justified because up to the early eighties the decline in developing countries' economic growth was rather small on an average (Agarwal, Glismann, Nunnenkamp, 1983). In addition, it is hardly possible to decide how much of loss in growth was attributable to restrictive domestic policies on the one hand, and to exogenous factors on the other. The balance of payments effect of changes in import ratios was calculated by deducting hypothetical import volumes from actual trade figures. Hypothetical imports for 1974–82 were estimated by applying historical income elasticities of import demand[1] to real GDP figures of 1974–82.

Results presented in Table 25 show that import ratios were only slightly reduced on an average of all NOPECs. Not more than $15 billion were saved in this way, which equalled 1.4 per cent of total real imports in 1974–81 or 3.3 per cent of long-term debt outstanding in 1981. At the beginning of the period under consideration, actual imports even exceeded hypothetical figures. Most developing countries seem to have been rather reluctant in restricting imports. Later on, however, strong differences emerged between individual countries[2]. Focusing on aggregated differences between actual and hypothetical imports relative to total imports in 1974–82, three groups can be identified. For the first group—including Chile, Indonesia, the Ivory Coast, Malaysia, the Philippines and Turkey—the development of imports was by and large in line with earlier patterns. In seven countries forming the second group—Argentina, Colombia, Egypt, India, Mexico, Nigeria, Venezuela—domestic policies resulted in import volumes which were at least 6 per cent higher than figures predicted under constant policy conditions. Sharply contrasting with these two groups, imports were significantly constrained (by at least 25 per cent) in Brazil, Korea, Thailand, Yugoslavia and Zaire.

It is striking that each group consists of both problem and

Table 25: Balance of Payments Impact of Domestic Import Policies of Major Third World Borrowing Countries, 1974–82[a] (in billions of US$)

	1974	1975	1976	1977	1978	1979	1980	1981	1982	Σ 1974–82[b]		
										billions of US$	as percent of total imports	as percent of external debt
All NOPECs	4.89	0.85	-4.89	-4.15	-1.70	-0.85	-6.27	-2.87	n.a.	-14.99	-1.4	-3.3
Argentina	0.18	0.23	-0.43	-0.04	-0.37	0.35	1.18	0.90	n.a.	2.00	8.9	8.4
Brazil	2.01	0.22	-1.14	-2.51	-2.76	-3.05	-4.64	-5.12	n.a.	-16.99	-24.8	-26.3
Chile	0.03	-0.25	-0.12	0.04	0.25	0.27	-0.02	0.15	n.a.	0.35	3.2	2.9
Colombia	0.00	-0.19	-0.15	-0.07	0.14	0.12	0.60	0.67	n.a.	1.12	8.7	18.7
Egypt	0.36	1.13	0.92	1.19	1.78	-0.22	n.a.	n.a.	n.a.	5.16	36.1	42.3
India	0.27	0.02	-0.31	0.16	0.31	0.33	0.89	n.a.	n.a.	1.67	6.2	9.3
Indonesia	0.43	0.64	0.92	0.44	-0.21	-1.03	-0.81	-0.43	n.a.	-0.05	-0.2	-0.3
Ivory Coast	-0.07	-0.02	-0.12	0.01	0.23	n.a.	n.a.	n.a.	n.a.	0.03	0.6	1.0
Rep. of Korea	-1.57	-2.58	-3.97	-5.13	-6.31	-7.84	-7.79	-9.56	-11.78	-56.53	-83.7	-257.0
Malaysia	0.00	-0.58	-0.61	-0.56	-0.23	0.02	0.27	-0.05	0.40	-1.34	-4.1	-43.3[c]
Mexico	0.62	0.47	-0.12	-0.70	-0.50	0.66	2.71	4.48	n.a.	7.62	16.4	14.3
Nigeria	0.30	2.50	3.91	5.42	5.58	3.12	5.33	7.47	n.a.	33.63	68.3	560.5
Philippines	-0.02	-0.03	-0.01	-0.19	0.11	0.19	0.15	-0.18	-0.01	0.01	0.0	0.1
Thailand	-0.38	-0.71	-0.94	-0.83	-1.08	-0.98	-1.15	-1.47	-2.12	-9.66	-45.5	-103.3[d]
Turkey	0.44	0.55	0.61	0.49	-0.34	-0.55	-0.56	-0.27	-0.33	0.04	0.2	0.3
Venezuela	-0.54	0.23	0.80	1.99	2.07	0.16	-0.64	-0.57	n.a.	3.50	11.2	23.5
Yugoslavia	-0.08	-0.54	-1.19	-1.34	-2.06	-2.46	-2.94	n.a.	n.a.	-10.61	-29.1	-70.3
Zaire	-0.04	-0.16	-0.28	-0.36	-0.36	-0.42	-0.40	-0.48	n.a.	-2.50	-75.3	-62.5[e]

[a] Actual minus hypothetical imports. A negative (positive) sign indicates an alleviation (deterioration) of balance of payments positions due to domestic import policies. For further details, see the text.

[b] For some countries, totals are for shorter periods. In these cases, ratios were calculated by referring to total merchandise imports in these shorter periods (instead of 1974–82) and long-term debt outstanding at the end of these shorter periods (instead of 1982), respectively, if not otherwise stated.

[c] Totals for 1974–80 relative to debt outstanding in 1980, because debt figures were not available later on.

[d] Totals for 1974–81 relative to debt outstanding in 1981.

non-problem borrowers. If the eighteen sample countries are ranked according to the balance of payments impact of import policies, ascribing rank one (eighteen) to the country with the greatest relative import reduction (increase), the average rank position of problem borrowers (9.5) is only slightly worse than the average position of sound debtor countries (8.2).[3] Accordingly, import policies alone cannot explain different experiences with foreign debt.

As already noted in Chapter 5, changes in developing countries' world-export-market shares as compared to the base period of 1970–73 may be attributed to domestic export policies. Actual export volumes of 1974–82 exceeding hypothetical figures (i.e. the product of market shares prevailing in the base period and actual export volumes of all world-market suppliers) point to a policy-induced easing of balance of payments pressures.[4] For all NOPECs this effect amounted to $78 billion in 1974–81, which equalled 8.4 per cent of total real exports in this period, or 17.3 per cent of long-term debt outstanding in 1981 (Table 26). Thus export policies seem to have had a far greater influence on the NOPECs' balance of payments position than import policies. This result is rather surprising. It could be expected that developing countries aiming at a quick adjustment to external disturbances would prefer to suppress imports because most protectionist measures are likely to become effective with only short delay, whereas export promotion policy-lags are probably longer.

In some cases, it may be that the success of developing countries in gaining world-market shares was largely due to longer-term outward-looking industrialisation strategies rather than to short-term adjustment measures. The most striking example in this respect was Korea, whose world-market shares rose steadily from 0.1 per cent in the mid-sixties to 1.6 per cent in 1982. In other countries, however, external shocks of the seventies seem to have provoked a re-orientation in export policies which significantly improved their balance of payments position, in spite of causation lags.[5] Argentina, Chile, the Philippines and Thailand may be mentioned as examples where the trend of declining

Table 26: Balance of Payments Impact of Domestic Export Policies of Major Third World Borrowing Countries, 1974–82[a] (in billions of US$)

	1974	1975	1976	1977	1978	1979	1980	1981	1982	Σ 1974–82[b]		
										billions of US$	as percent of total exports	as percent of external debt
All NOPECs	-1.44	3.85	2.65	0.45	5.66	10.20	21.50	35.41	n.a.	78.28	8.4	17.3
Argentina	-0.17	-0.68	0.18	1.71	2.15	1.60	0.86	1.90	n.a.	7.55	18.8	31.9
Brazil	0.42	0.99	0.41	-0.03	0.58	0.78	2.67	5.17	4.41	15.40	19.5	21.2
Chile	0.36	0.07	0.32	0.51	0.64	0.95	1.12	0.56	n.a.	4.53	22.5	38.1
Colombia	-0.19	-0.13	-0.48	-0.58	-0.25	-0.22	-0.16	-0.40	-0.26	-2.67	-25.0	-40.2[c]
Egypt	-0.45	-0.47	-0.47	-0.55	-0.56	-0.78	-0.51	-0.46	n.a.	-4.25	-55.3	-28.3
India	-0.02	0.12	0.72	0.48	0.24	0.25	-0.14	n.a.	n.a.	1.65	5.8	9.2
Indonesia	0.56	0.22	0.34	0.68	0.76	0.28	0.04	0.12	n.a.	3.00	10.0	17.3
Ivory Coast	0.10	0.06	0.14	-0.06	-0.03	-0.11	0.04	0.09	n.a.	0.23	3.0	5.1[d]
Rep. of Korea	1.41	2.15	3.46	3.73	5.35	5.07	5.83	7.48	8.31	42.79	64.0	194.5
Malaysia	-0.34	-0.21	0.14	0.03	0.31	0.33	0.19	0.17	0.81	1.43	4.2	11.5[e]
Mexico	-0.20	-0.33	-0.23	0.13	0.84	1.89	4.00	6.93	n.a.	13.03	35.6	24.4
Nigeria	-0.13	-0.94	-0.82	-0.88	-1.32	-1.27	-1.79	-2.70	-2.68	-12.53	-49.0	-156.6
Philippines	-0.23	-0.11	0.15	0.51	0.33	0.40	0.91	0.96	1.25	4.17	17.3	34.2
Thailand	0.08	0.01	0.47	0.73	0.85	0.95	1.02	1.54	2.23	7.88	30.5	77.4[c]
Turkey	-0.07	-0.09	0.14	-0.19	0.02	-0.33	-0.25	0.85	1.67	1.75	12.1	11.7
Venezuela	-1.91	-2.82	-3.45	-3.91	-4.26	-4.40	-5.16	-5.34	-5.19	-36.44	-146.5	-218.2
Yugoslavia	-0.05	-0.10	0.01	-0.31	-0.45	-0.80	-0.40	n.a.	n.a.	-2.10	-9.5	-13.9
Zaire	-0.13	-0.25	-0.47	-0.56	-0.63	-0.65	-0.54	-1.04	n.a.	-4.27	-60.6	-106.8[d]

[a] Actual minus hypothetical exports. A positive (negative) sign indicates an alleviation (deterioration) of balance of payments positions due to domestic export policies. For further details, see the text.

[b] For some countries. totals are for 1974–81 or 1974–80 only. In these cases, ratios were calculated on the basis of total merchandise exports in 1974–81 or 1974–80 (instead of 1974–82) and long-term debt outstanding in 1981 or 1980 (instead of 1982), respectively, if not otherwise stated.

[c] Totals for 1974–81 relative to debt outstanding in 1981, because debt figures were not available for 1982.

[d] Totals for 1974–81 relative to public and publicly guaranteed debt outstanding in 1981.

market shares prevailing in the sixties and early seventies was reversed after 1973.[6]

Relative to total real exports in 1974–82, export gains were greatest in Korea (64 per cent), Mexico (36 per cent; for a qualification, see n. 6) and Thailand (31 per cent). They were followed by four countries—Chile, Brazil, Argentina and the Philippines—for which additional export volumes of about 20 per cent were calculated. In five more countries, actual exports outpaced hypothetical figures by between 3 and 12 per cent (in descending order: Turkey, Indonesia, India, Malaysia and the Ivory Coast). Only six countries failed in reducing balance of payments deficits via a policy-induced export expansion—Yugoslavia, Colombia, Nigeria, Egypt, Zaire, Venezuela. The export shortfall was most noteworthy in the two last mentioned cases, amounting to 145 per cent (Venezuela) and 61 per cent (Zaire) of aggregated actual exports.

Country-specific calculations underline that the borrowing countries' balance of payments strains were primarily eased on the export side. Against only five countries for which significant import reductions were reported, export gains of 10 per cent and more could be observed in nine out of eighteen borrowers. Nevertheless, as in the case of imports, there is only a loose connection, if any, between export performance on the one hand and the foreign debt situation on the other. Indeed, Venezuela and Zaire, which experienced the greatest export losses, both belonged to the group of problem borrowers. At the other extreme, Korea and Thailand, which benefited most from additional exports, proved to be rather sound debtors. In between, however, the evidence was confusing. Problem countries like Argentina, Brazil and Chile showed a fairly favourable export performance, contrasting with Colombia, for example, which had no difficulties in servicing foreign debt, although it continued to lose world-market shares.

Possibly, the impact of short-term adjustment measures in the field of external trade was dominated by more fundamental economic factors like the degree of the government's direct involvement in the economy, the investment climate, the stability of domestic currency etc. Generally speaking, the internal use of funds borrowed abroad is critical for preventing future difficulties in servicing foreign debt.[7] No problems are to be expected, provided the yield of externally financed projects exceeds the interest rate attached to the loan. This is why a consumptive use of funds is most likely to cause repayment problems later on.

Governments of some developing countries, in particular, seem to have raised foreign loans for consumptive purposes in the past. In countries like Venezuela, 'state agencies fell into the habit of borrowing short term for almost everything ... They also borrowed to finance their operating deficits'. (Greiff, Martin, 1981). Probably, government expenditures contributed significantly to rising balance of payments deficits and augmenting external financing requirements (for government expenditure shares, see Table 27). Expenditures for military purposes or infrastructural projects, for example, typically imply considerable imports of foreign systems, technologies and machinery. Budget deficits, prevailing in almost all countries under consideration (Table 28), may have further enlarged balance of payments troubles (Sjaastad, 1983, p. 315). Especially in the case of rising budget deficits, fiscal policies are likely to induce (additional) inflationary pressures, either by financing deficits via excessive money creation or by crowding-out a more productive utilisation of funds. Moreover, countries heavily relying on centralised bureaucratic decision-making run considerable risks of great mistakes which cannot be corrected by competition, that is, by the self-correcting mechanism implicit in a great number of independent decisions by private economic agents (Meltzer, 1983; Glismann, Nunnenkamp, 1983).

The government's share in domestic absorption and rising budget deficits, therefore, may be regarded as important variables in explaining debt problems (Khan, Knight, 1983). Actually, Table 27 shows that government expenditure shares were higher for problem borrowers (21 per cent, on an average, in 1970–82) than for sound debtors (17.8 per cent). Moreover, in the former group, six out of eight members experienced rising budget deficits after 1973, whereas in the latter group, deficits were reduced in three

Table 27: Government Expenditure Shares in Domestic Absorption of Major Third World Borrowing Countries, 1970–82[a] (in percent)

	1970–82[b]	1970–73	1974–78	1979–82[b]		1970–82[b]	1970–73	1974–78	1979–82[b]
Argentina	18.0	17.2	18.5	18.4	Malaysia	29.5	24.4	28.5	35.9
Brazil	9.2	9.9	9.3	8.4	Mexico	13.9	11.4	14.8	16.8
Chile	29.2	32.2[c]	29.3	27.3	Nigeria	17.7	12.2	23.2[e]	n.a.
Colombia	12.2	12.5[d]	11.7	12.9	Philippines	14.2	11.9	16.8	13.3
Egypt	n.a.	n.a.	n.a.	n.a.	Thailand	16.2	16.8	15.4	16.7
India	11.6	10.6	12.2	13.1	Turkey	21.8	21.7	21.8	n.a.
Indonesia	19.7	15.0	20.2	27.5	Venezuela	23.4	20.0	25.2	25.2
Ivory Coast	n.a.	n.a.	n.a.	n.a.	Yugoslavia	20.7	22.1	22.2	16.4
Rep. of Korea	15.7	15.2	15.3	17.2	Zaire	32.1	36.1	31.3	28.3

[a] Period averages.
[b] For many countries, calculations are for shorter periods because of missing data.
[c] 1973.
[d] 1971–73.
[e] 1975 excluded because of missing data.

Source: IMF, *International Financial Statistics.*

Table 28: Share of Governments' Budget Deficits in Domestic Absorption of Major Third World Borrowing Countries, 1970–82ᵃ (in percent)

	1970–82ᵇ	1970–73	1974–78	1979–82ᵇ		1970–82ᵇ	1970–73	1974–78	1979–82ᵇ
Argentina	-4.48	-3.42	-5.87	-3.09	Malaysia	-9.43	-6.67	-8.00	-13.99
Brazil	0.01	-0.16	0.14	0.03	Mexico	-3.14	-2.28	-3.81	-3.19
Chile	-0.18	-6.77ᶜ	-0.97	5.04	Nigeria	0.73	0.93	0.52ᵈ	n.a.
Colombia	-0.63	-1.83	0.18	-0.25	Philippines	-0.87	0.25	-0.59	-2.35
Egypt	n.a.	n.a.	n.a.	n.a.	Thailand	-3.10	-3.83	-2.37	-3.28
India	-4.37	-3.61	-4.63	-6.14	Turkey	-2.70	-2.42	-2.92	n.a.
Indonesia	-1.68	-2.44	-1.06	-1.68	Venezuela	-1.52	-0.44	-2.60	-1.16
Ivory Coast	n.a.	n.a.	n.a.	n.a.	Yugoslavia	-1.26	-1.05	-1.76	-0.69
Rep. of Korea	-1.76	-1.32	-1.67	-2.48	Zaire	-7.70	-6.06	-11.37	-3.78

ᵃ Period averages; negative (positive) sign in case of budget deficit (surplus).
ᵇ For many countries, calculations are for shorter periods because of missing data.
ᶜ 1973.
ᵈ 1975 excluded because of missing data.

Source: IMF, *International Financial Statistics.*

out of five cases (Table 28). Both results support the hypothesis that the probability of debt problems has been enhanced by relatively strong governmental economic interferences through fiscal policies.

Because of the above-mentioned risks arising out of a consumptive use of funds borrowed abroad, it may be supposed that a high investment ratio will be an important safeguard against difficulties in servicing foreign debt (Sachs, 1982). Surprisingly, however, average shares of gross fixed capital formation in domestic absorption were slightly above 20 per cent in 1970–82 for both the sound debtor group and the problem-borrower group (Table 29). On the other hand, the expected relationship can be observed with respect to the *change* in investment ratios after 1973. All three countries reporting declining average investment ratios in 1974–82 (Zaire and, to a considerably lesser degree, also Brazil and Chile) could be labelled as problem borrowers. In addition, the increase in investment ratios remained comparatively small for the remaining five countries in this category.

This somewhat ambiguous evidence points to an important qualification which has to be made in using investment ratios as an explaining variable for debt problems. An investive use of foreign loans, certainly, is essential for avoiding future repayment difficulties, but high investments cannot be regarded as a sufficient condition in this respect. Investments may fail in generating a surplus high enough for transferring debt-service payments falling due. Besides the level of investments, it is crucial that the industrialisation strategy pursued is in line with the country's comparative advantages. Developing countries typically characterised by abundant labour supply and relatively scarce capital are well advised to concentrate on labour-intensive projects. It is in this latter respect that many failures and mis-specialisations seem to have occurred. Some borrowers were keen to install large capital-intensive plants; for example, steel mills, petrochemical plants and other heavy industries. They also tried to quickly build up advanced infrastructural facilities like nuclear power plants or underground railways. Frequently, significant parts of projects like these were financed exter-

Table 29: Investment Ratios of Major Third World Borrowing Countries, 1970–82[a] (in percent)

	1970–82[b]	1970–73	1974–78	1979–82[b]		1970–82[b]	1970–73	1974–78	1979–82[b]
Argentina	23.3	20.3	25.5	23.8	Malaysia	26.3	22.0	26.1	30.8
Brazil	21.5	21.6	22.3	19.9	Mexico	20.4	18.8	20.3	23.5
Chile	12.8	12.9[c]	10.9	15.2	Nigeria	22.6	17.7	26.5	n.a.
Colombia	19.7	19.0	19.4	21.2	Philippines	20.9	15.9	22.0	24.5
Egypt	17.5	11.3	19.6	21.4	Thailand	22.4	21.5	22.2	23.4
India	17.3	16.0	18.2	18.5	Turkey	18.4	17.1	19.5	n.a.
Indonesia	19.5	16.3	19.7	23.5	Venezuela	28.0	24.4	31.5	27.0
Ivory Coast	23.0	21.0	24.6	n.a.	Yugoslavia	31.3	29.6	32.2	32.1
Rep. of Korea	24.9	21.3	24.9	28.6	Zaire	22.3	25.1	23.1	17.2

[a] Share of gross fixed capital formation in domestic absorption; period averages.
[b] For many countries, calculations are for shorter periods because of missing data.
[c] 1973.

Source: IMF, *International Financial Statistics.*

nally. Although available information is rather casual, it seems that especially in problem countries like Brazil, Mexico, Venezuela and Yugoslavia, industrialisation strategies were largely in conflict with comparative advantages. Difficulties in servicing foreign debt became even more probable if—as in the case of Venezuela—projects with long gestation periods were financed short-term (Greiff, Martin, 1981).

Not only fiscal policies, but also monetary policies in developing countries could be expected to have an impact on their foreign debt situation. Permissive monetary policies, resulting in relatively high inflation rates, will increase the amount of capital imports required for compensating enlarged current-account deficits. This is because rising differentials in domestic and international purchasing-power developments will induce an import expansion and, simultaneously, reduce world-market competitiveness of the country's exports, provided that differentials are not fully offset by an appropriate devaluation of the domestic currency. Evidence presented in Table 30 strongly supports this reasoning. Actually, annual average inflation rates for problem borrowers in 1973–82 (57.6 per cent) were more than four times as high as for sound debtors (13.7 per cent). The difference between both country groups remains considerable, even if Latin American members of the former group (traditionally characterised by extremely high inflation rates) are left out of account. For the three non-Latin-American problem borrowers—Turkey, Yugoslavia, Zaire—an average inflation rate of 37.4 per cent is calculated.

Considering exchange-rate policies,[8] it is striking that in only eight countries nominal devaluations in 1974–82 were high enough to fully offset unfavourable developments in inflation differentials, as indicated by figures above 100 in Table 31.[9] In this respect, however, hardly any difference is to be observed for problem borrowers on the one hand and sound debtors on the other. In the former group, Turkey, Yugoslavia and, particularly, Zaire reported notable real appreciations, as did Colombia and Indonesia in the latter group, comparing average exchange rates of 1974–82 with

Table 30: Inflation Rates for Major Third World Borrowing Countries, 1973–82 (in percent)[a]

	1973–82	1973–78	1978–82		1973–82	1973–78	1978–82
Argentina	152.3	163.5	139.0	Malaysia	6.6	6.7	6.4
Brazil	57.4	35.8	89.4	Mexico	25.5	22.0	30.1
Chile	102.5	199.6	24.1	Nigeria	17.5	21.5	12.6
Colombia	25.5	25.6	25.4	Philippines	14.5	13.9	15.2
Egypt	11.3	10.7	12.1	Thailand	10.1	10.0	10.2
India	9.0	7.0	11.4	Turkey	38.1	25.4	56.0
Indonesia	17.5	19.2	15.4	Venezuela	11.1	8.2	14.8
Ivory Coast	14.2	16.1	11.8	Yugoslavia	22.9	16.9	30.8
Republic of Korea	19.8	19.7	20.1	Zaire	51.1	49.5	53.1

a Period averages. Wholesale prices where available; consumer prices otherwise.

Source: IMF, *International Financial Statistics.*

Table 31: Real Exchange Rates of Major Third World Borrowing Countries, 1974–82 (1970–73 = 100)[a]

	1974–82	1974–78	1979–82		1974–82	1974–78	1979–82
Argentina	99.4	109.1	87.2	Malaysia	111.3	104.5	120.0
Brazil	116.6	112.0	122.4	Mexico	102.5	103.1	101.8
Chile	218.4	218.0	218.8	Nigeria	69.0	77.6	58.3
Colombia	85.8	90.8	79.6	Philippines	87.0	89.3	84.3
Egypt	136.0	108.4	170.7	Thailand	102.2	101.6	102.9
India	119.3	114.3	125.6	Turkey	93.6	88.1	100.4
Indonesia	81.1	75.2	88.4	Venezuela	106.4	111.5	100.0
Ivory Coast	85.5	92.1	77.4	Yugoslavia	93.3	93.2	93.4
Republic of Korea	96.5	100.4	91.5	Zaire	60.0	66.2	52.2

[a] Period averages. Figures above (below) 100 indicate a real devaluation (appreciation) of national currencies vis-à-vis major trading partners as compared to the period 1970–73; for further details, see the text.

Source: IMF, *International Financial Statistics.*

those of the early seventies. Remarkable differences, however, existed with respect to the steadiness and predictability of exchange-rate developments (Table 32). On an average, annual variations in real exchange rates were significantly higher for problem borrowers (12 per cent) than for sound debtors (8 per cent). This seems important because heavy short-term fluctuations, which are hardly foreseeable, may considerably complicate both production and investment calculations of private economic agents. Uncertainties arising out of unsteady exchange-rate policies are likely to impede the achievement of stable external trade relations and are detrimental to the country's international competitiveness, thereby giving rise to further external financing needs.

Policies analysed above can be considered to have strongly influenced economic growth in developing countries. This is not to ignore that the Third World's growth performance may have been affected by external factors too. The striking uniformity of declining growth rates after 1978 may, in particular, be attributed to factors outside the control of developing countries (for the eighteen sample countries, real growth was reduced from 5.5 per cent in 1973–78 to 3.2 per cent in 1978–82; Table 33). The strong differences in growth rates within the sample, however, are supposed to be largely due to domestic policies pursued. This reasoning is supported by evidence presented in the preceding chapter. According to this, fast growing countries like Korea and Thailand were also severely hit by external shocks. On the other hand, the growth performance was very poor in countries like Argentina and Zaire, although external disturbances remained relatively modest for them. The same applies to Nigeria, which even derived benefits from external shocks.

A favourable growth performance seems to be the best safeguard against debt problems (de Vries, 1983b, p. 16). Though at a rather global level, high economic growth rates indicate that borrowed funds were used productively, thereby improving the country's ability to service foreign loans. This, in turn, may motivate commercial banks to continue lending to the country, which minimises the threat of a sudden shortage of foreign capital supplies. The pattern of growth

Table 32: Annual Changes in Real Exchange Rates of Major Third World Borrowing Countries, 1974–82 (in percent)

	1974	1975	1976	1977	1978	1979	1980	1981	1982	Average in absolute annual fluctuations in 1974–82
Argentina	1.8	50.9	−34.7	27.3	−9.9	−26.2	−11.8	13.9	61.4	26.4
Brazil	0.5	3.0	−1.1	1.9	4.4	6.1	6.4	−19.1	16.2	6.6
Chile	42.5	27.0	−5.5	−10.2	17.6	−0.1	0.4	−18.6	5.8	14.2
Colombia	−5.9	4.5	−5.4	−9.8	2.3	−3.4	0.8	−5.7	−6.4	4.9
Egypt	−0.4	2.0	−2.0	−0.6	−0.3	82.6	−9.8	−7.4	−10.6	11.7
India	−3.7	7.9	12.1	−0.2	7.8	0.7	−5.2	0.6	3.2	4.6
Indonesia	−14.2	−11.7	−17.8	3.4	17.6	22.9	−2.7	−7.2	−10.7	12.0
Ivory Coast	2.5	−5.7	0.2	−13.4	−4.8	−6.4	−2.7	6.3	8.7	5.6
Republic of Korea	−14.6	1.6	−5.1	1.3	4.0	−10.7	1.6	−1.7	−1.2	4.6
Malaysia	0.0	1.4	4.5	1.1	4.2	0.4	7.1	15.8	−19.2	6.0
Mexico	−3.8	−1.0	5.0	11.5	−3.7	−5.0	−8.7	−8.6	44.7	10.2
Nigeria	−3.5	−16.2	−17.6	−5.4	−3.7	−0.3	−5.3	−10.3	0.4	7.0
Philippines	−18.5	8.6	−0.2	2.3	8.8	−8.7	−4.0	−2.9	−6.5	6.7
Thailand	−7.5	3.5	1.0	2.7	9.2	−3.4	−5.6	−0.4	−1.2	3.8
Turkey	−10.4	4.0	−4.7	−3.4	2.5	−15.4	44.0	1.0	7.4	10.3
Venezuela	8.5	0.6	−3.3	−1.0	1.3	0.4	−6.1	−7.9	−7.3	4.0
Yugoslavia	−6.0	−1.7	−5.0	−3.2	2.9	−3.4	11.5	−8.2	7.0	5.4
Zaire	−8.9	−12.7	−11.2	−31.5	−24.4	13.1	30.0	7.3	−8.2	16.4

Source: IMF, *International Financial Statistics.*

Table 33: Average Annual Growth in Real GDP for Major Third World Borrowing Countries, 1973–82 (in percent)

	1973–82	1973–78	1978–82		1973–82	1973–78	1978–82
Argentina	0.5	1.6	1.0	Malaysia	7.0	7.0	7.1
Brazil	5.7[a]	7.0	3.6[a]	Mexico	5.8	5.5	6.3
Chile	1.5	1.6	1.4	Nigeria	0.5	1.3	-0.4
Colombia	4.9[a]	5.5	3.9[a]	Philippines	5.5	6.3	4.6
Egypt	8.9[b]	8.9	8.7[b]	Thailand	6.8	7.7	5.6
India	4.0[a]	5.1	2.2[a]	Turkey	4.1	5.4	2.5
Indonesia	6.9	7.2	6.5	Venezuela	3.3	6.0	0.0
Ivory Coast	5.7[b]	7.8	-4.2[b]	Yugoslavia	5.3[a]	6.3	3.6[a]
Republic of Korea	7.4	10.3	3.9	Zaire	-1.0	-2.4	0.8

[a] 1973–81 and 1978–81, respectively.
[b] 1973–79 and 1978–79, respectively.

Source: IMF, *International Financial Statistics.*

differences within the sample emerging from Table 33 is therefore hardly surprising. For the sound debtor group, real economic growth rates in 1973–82 (5.9 per cent) were nearly twice as high as for the problem-borrower group (3.2 per cent). This discrepancy was further enlarged in 1978–82 because the *relative* reduction in growth rates was comparatively sharp for the latter group (from 3.9 per cent in 1973–78 to 2.4 per cent in 1978–82; the respective figures for five sound debtors stood at 6.5 per cent and 5.1 per cent).

Summing up the evidence presented above, it can be concluded that domestic policies had a clear impact on the foreign debt situation of developing countries. The observation that some countries faced no major problems in servicing external debt, whereas others ran into serious difficulties, can at least partly be attributed to the degree to which governments of borrowing countries succeeded in adjusting to external shocks and in bringing about economic conditions which can be regarded as well suited to prevent international indebtedness from deteriorating.

Table 34 summarises the analysis of domestic policies. First, the eighteen sample countries are ranked according to the performance in different policy areas. In each column, rank one (eighteen) is given to the country with the performance regarded as most (least) conducive to avoiding debt problems. Second, an average rank position is calculated for each country under consideration (see the last column of Table 34). Finally, average rank positions for eight problem borrowers and five sound debtors are presented at the bottom of Table 34.

With regard to overall economic policies, the average rank position of the former group is 10.4, against 8.3 for the latter group. This supports the hypothesis that countries facing major debt problems may be characterised by a relatively unfavourable policy performance. The difference of slightly more than two rank positions is, however, too small to consider policies pursued by non-problem borrowers as optional. Actually, their performance was no better in all respects. A comparison of the degree in export expansion and of the development in real exchange rates revealed only marginal differences between problem and

Table 34: Ranking of Major Third World Borrowing Countries According to Domestic Policy Performance[a]

	Import reduction[b] (1 = highest)	Export expansion[c] (1 = highest)	Government expenditure shares[d] (1 = lowest)	Shares of governments' budget deficits[d] (1 = lowest)	Change in shares of governments' budget deficits[e] (1 = greatest reduction of deficits)	Investment ratios[d] (1 = highest)
Argentina	14	6	9	14	14	5
Brazil	5	5	1	2	5	10
Chile	11	4	14	3	1	18
Colombia	13	14	3	4	2	13
Egypt	17	16	n.a.	n.a.	n.a.	16
India	12	10	2	13	10	17
Indonesia	7	9	10	8	3	14
Ivory Coast	10	12	n.a.	n.a.	n.a.	6
Rep. of Korea	1	1	6	9	9	4
Malaysia	6	11	15	16	16	3
Mexico	16	2	4	12	11	12
Nigeria	18	15	8	1	7	7
Philippines	8	7	5	5	12.5	11
Thailand	3	3	7	11	4	8
Turkey	9	8	12	10	8	15
Venezuela	15	18	13	7	12.5	2
Yugoslavia	4	13	11	6	6	1
Zaire	2	17	16	15	15	9
Average rank positions:						
Problem borrowers[j]	9.5	9.1	10.0	8.6	9.1	9.0
Non-problem borrowers[k]	8.2	9.4	7.4	10.4	7.0	11.0

[a] In each column, rank '1' is given to the country with the performance regarded as best suited for avoiding debt problems; accordingly, rank '18' is given to the country with the worst performance.
[b] Aggregated reduction in 1974–82, relative to total imports in 1974–82.
[c] Aggregated expansion in 1974–82, relative to total exports in 1974–82.
[d] Average share in domestic absorption for 1970–82.
[e] Change (in percentage points) in 1974–82 vis-à-vis 1970–73.

Source: Tables 25–33.

Table 34 (continued): Ranking of Major Third World Borrowing Countries According to Domestic Policy Performance[a]

	Change in investment ratios[f] (1 = highest increase)	Inflation rates[g] (1 = lowest)	Real exchange rates[h] (1 = highest depreciation)	Fluctuations of real exchange rates[i] (1 = lowest)	Growth rates[g] (1 = highest)	Average rank position
Argentina	7	18	9	18	17	11.9
Brazil	17	16	4	9	8	7.5
Chile	16	17	1	16	15	10.5
Colombia	15	12.5	14	5	11	9.7
Egypt	1	5	2	14	1	9.0
India	10.5	2	3	3.5	13	8.7
Indonesia	4	8.5	16	15	4	9.0
Ivory Coast	9	6	15	7	7	9.0
Rep. of Korea	6	10	10	3.5	2	5.6
Malaysia	5	1	5	8	3	8.1
Mexico	12	12.5	7	12	6	9.7
Nigeria	2	8.5	17	11	16	10.0
Philippines	3	7	13	10	9	8.2
Thailand	14	3	8	1	5	6.1
Turkey	10.5	14	11	13	12	11.1
Venezuela	8	4	6	2	14	9.2
Yugoslavia	13	11	12	6	10	8.5
Zaire	18	15	18	17	18	14.5
Average rank positions:						
Problem borrowers[j]	12.7	13.4	8.5	11.6	12.5	10.4
Non-problem borrowers[k]	9.7	5.4	9.2	6.5	7.2	8.3

f Change (in percent) in 1974–82 vis-à-vis 1970–73.
g Period averages for 1973–82.
h 1974–82 vis-à-vis 1970–73.
i Absolute averages in 1974–82.
j Argentina, Brazil, Chile, Mexico, Turkey, Venezuela, Yugoslavia and Zaire.
k Colombia, India, Indonesia, Malaysia and Thailand.

Source: Tables 25–33.

non-problem borrowers. The ranking of the second group was even significantly worse with respect to governments' budget deficits and investment ratios. On the other hand, advantages of the sound debtor group were most remarkable with regards to inflation rates, real economic growth and the steadiness of exchange rate policy. The same applies to import reductions, government expenditure shares, the change in governments' budget deficits and the change in investment ratios, though to a considerably lesser extent.

NOTES

1. A very simple import function was used, with real GDP as the only exogenous variable determining real imports. Relative prices of domestic vis-à-vis foreign goods were neglected because this variable remained insignificant in former calculations (for further details, *see* Agarwal, Glismann, Nunnenkamp, 1983). The regression was run using data for 1962–73 in most cases. For some countries estimates resulted in insignificant elasticities. In these cases hypothetical import volumes were calculated on the basis of average import/GDP ratios prevailing in the early seventies.

2. This statement remains valid even if extremes on both sides are left out of account. For countries like Korea and Nigeria, the calculations of hypothetical imports may be distorted by atypically high or low income elasticities of import demand prevailing in the base period (Korea, 2.3 and Nigeria, 0.6, against an average of 1.2 for all NOPECs), the normalisation of which probably cannot be fully attributed to short-term adjustment policies.

3. Referring to results arrived at in Chapter 4, Argentina, Brazil, Chile, Mexico, Turkey, Venezuela, Yugoslavia and Zaire are considered as problem borrowers, as opposed to Colombia, India, Indonesia, Malaysia and Thailand, which could be labelled as sound debtors (the remaining five countries lying in between).

4. For a more detailed discussion of export policies, *see* de Vries, 1983a.

5. The observation that in 1974 and 1975 the large majority of sample countries still experienced export losses (indicated by negative-signed figures in Table 26), whereas export gains dominated later on, points to causation lags.

6. A similar development in market shares took place in Mexico. In this case, however, the change must be largely attributed to oil findings which boosted exports since the late seventies, rather than to export policy measures.

7.　For an in-depth analysis, *see* Avramovic *et al.*, 1964. An empirical application of the so-called critical interest-rate approach was recently presented in Lee, 1983.

8.　The relationship between developments in exchange rates and the emergence of debt problems is stressed in Aliber, 1980.

9.　Real exchange rates presented in Table 31 are calculated in the following way. As a first step, nominal exchange rates for the countries under consideration vis-à-vis the five most important trading partners, both on the export and on the import side (weighted with the partners' shares in the country's total external trade in the early seventies), are calculated. Second, nominal exchange rates are deflated by an index of relative prices which compares domestic inflation with inflation prevailing in trading partner countries.

7   Imprudent Lending by Commercial Banks?

It is relatively easy to explain why Third World countries have increasingly appeared on international capital markets in the last decade. The unfavourable economic environment has posed a major threat to their further economic development. Adjustment to worsening world-market conditions has often been impeded by harmful domestic policies. The NOPECs' mounting demand for foreign funds has not been matched by a sufficient supply of official development aid in the form of outright grants or subsidised credits. Accordingly, NOPECs have had to rely on private capital on a far larger scale than ever before. The rise in foreign indebtedness of developing countries might have been substantially narrowed if international commercial banks had refused to meet the Third World's demands. In other words, the emergence of debt problems was probably not the sole responsibility of borrowers. The hypothesis of this chapter is that problems might also have been avoided by more prudential lending policies of banks.

The question of whether the behaviour of commercial banks in the seventies gave rise to widespread difficulties in servicing foreign debt is far more difficult to check than hypotheses analysed before. Why is it that banks were so eager to channel huge amounts of capital to the Third World? Why were funds largely allocated to countries which later on declared default? Is it that banks were not aware of the risks involved or may it be even that private creditors disregarded risks because they were confident that possible losses would be socialised by officially bailing out private banks? Questions like these are hard to be tackled empirically. Therefore, the following analysis will concentrate on a statistical presentation of international bank lending to Third World borrowers and a somewhat tentative assessment of underlying factors and plausible explanations of bank behaviour.

In mid-1983, gross long-term and short-term debt of NOPECs vis-à-vis BIS reporting banks stood at $252 billion (Table 35). Within ten years gross figures had increased eightfold (i.e. by little less than 30 per cent per annum) as compared to an overall annual capital market growth of 24 per cent. The market share of NOPECs remained comparatively low throughout the whole period under consideration, just touching 15 per cent in the early eighties. Yet it cannot be concluded that NOPECs played a negligible role in international bank lending becaue totals in Table 35 include all interbank positions. By netting out interbank transactions between banks within the BIS reporting area (i.e. adjusting for double-counting), overall market volumes are reduced by about 40 per cent.[1] In this net Euromarket definition,[2] nearly 25 per cent of banks' claims held in 1980–82 were accounted for by NOPECs. Moreover, net of borrowing countries' deposits in the Euromarket, NOPECs formed by far the largest debtor group. In 1983 banks' net claims on them fell only slightly short of $150 billion, whereas other net borrowing country groups, such as the developed economies outside the reporting area and the Eastern European countries, owed only $65 and $34 billion, respectively, on a net basis.[3]

Banks' claims on NOPECs were highly concentrated on Latin American borrowers. On a gross basis their share steadily exceeded 65 per cent. Adjusted for the developing countries' deposits in the Euromarket, the exposure of commercial banks in different Third World regions was even more unbalanced. In Africa—where already gross figures remaind negligible—and particularly in Asia, gross debt due to banks was largely matched by deposits. For Latin America, however, deposits further declined from an already low level of 38 per cent of gross liabilities in the seventies to less than 25 per cent in the early eighties. Consequently, Latin America accounted for more than 90 per cent of net bank assets vis-à-vis all NOPECs.[4]

A significant portion of the developing countries' bank debt has been raised via syndicated bank loans. According

Table 35: International Claims of BIS Reporting Banks on Different Groups of Countries, 1973–83 (in billions of US$)[a]

| | | Reporting area[b] | | Non-oil developing countries[c] | | | | | | | |
	Total	gross[d]	net[d]	Total gross[d]	Total net[d]	Latin America gross[d]	Latin America net[d]	Asia gross[d]	Asia net[d]	Africa gross[d]	Africa net[d]
1973	296.0	n.a.	n.a.	32.0	4.5	n.a.	n.a.	n.a.	n.a.	n.a.	n.a.
1974	361.0	n.a.	n.a.	47.0	15.5	n.a.	n.a.	n.a.	n.a.	n.a.	n.a.
1975	441.7	235.1	−35.0	63.0	26.3	43.5	27.2	12.9	2.5	3.3	−0.8
1976	547.4	269.5	−50.1	80.9	31.1	57.4	35.1	14.7	−0.2	4.4	−0.9
1977	689.7	349.9	−58.6	97.2	36.5	64.7	40.2	19.5	0.3	7.8	1.2
1978	893.1	467.5	−66.8	119.9	44.1	79.1	46.6	22.9	0.7	11.3	4.0
1979	1 111.0	588.2	−97.7	155.7	67.1	102.5	64.8	31.1	5.1	14.3	5.1
1980	1 321.9	704.4	−119.7	193.3	101.9	129.2	93.2	38.4	11.1	15.9	6.1
1981	1 549.5	821.2	−129.8	229.6	131.5	158.3	118.6	42.8	13.4	16.9	7.0
1982	1 688.2	895.0	−130.8	247.2	146.2	169.2	132.3	47.1	12.7	18.0	9.2
1983[e]	1 689.0	885.5	−142.7	251.5	147.3	172.1	132.8	48.5	12.4	17.6	9.1

[a] Interbank lending included.
[b] Group of Ten countries plus Luxemburg, Switzerland, Denmark, Ireland and Austria.
[c] Excluded are: OPEC member countries, Bahrain, Brunei, Oman, Trinidad and Tobago and developing countries classified as offshore banking centres. The sum of figures for the three regions does not add up to the totals for all NOPECs because figures for the less important NOPECs located in the Middle East are not presented here.
[d] Gross: total (short- and long-term) assets of BIS reporting banks, in domestic and foreign currency, vis-à-vis borrowing country groups; net: gross figures minus total liabilities of banks vis-à-vis country groups.
[e] End of June.

Sources: BIS, *International Banking Developments*; BIS, *Annual Report*.

Table 36: International Medium- and Long-Term Bank Loans by Borrowing Country Group, 1973-83 (in billions of US$)

	Total	OECD countries	OPEC countries[a]	NOPECs	Eighteen major Third World borrowers[b]	Eight major problem borrowers[c]
1973	20.86	12.36	2.83	4.54	3.41	2.73
1974	28.54	18.29	0.81	7.41	6.26	4.23
1975	20.58	6.22	3.21	8.03	7.57	4.79
1976	27.92	9.90	3.40	10.97	10.64	7.66
1977	33.78	13.04	6.33	11.56	10.79	8.53
1978	65.81	30.37	9.72	21.84	23.59	15.76
1979	79.08	29.07	8.77	36.00	35.65	27.58
1980	79.92	41.16	6.84	28.16	27.56	19.34
1981	146.42	97.49	5.76	41.30	37.36	25.04
1982	97.66	55.07	9.02	31.35	32.25	22.49
1983[d]	67.46	32.93	6.34	25.59	23.46	15.21

[a] Included are also Bahrain, Oman and Trinidad and Tobago.
[b] For the list of borrowers included, see Chapter 3.
[c] According to evidence presented in Chapter 4, the following countries are regarded as problem borrowers in the Third World: Argentina, Brazil, Chile, Mexico, Turkey, Venezuela, Yugoslavia and Zaire.
[d] Estimates on the basis of data for January to November.

Source: OECD, *Financial Statistics*.

to Table 36, NOPECs absorbed a rising share of capital available in the medium-term and long-term Eurocurrency market for syndicated credits on a floating interest-rate basis. Whereas at the beginning of the period under consideration roughly a quarter of loans were raised by NOPECs, their share climbed to an average of 38 per cent in 1975-80. Gross lending of NOPECs amounted to $117 billion in this latter period. In the early eighties another $98 billion were borrowed.

The development of international bank lending to NOPECs in the seventies, as portrayed in Tables 35 and 36, probably was the result of a combination of supply and demand factors (Dennis, 1983; Fleming, Howson, 1980). After the first steep rise in oil prices in 1973/74 most OPEC countries were unable to spend total extra oil revenues for additional imports immediately. Searching for high-yielding financial investment opportunities abroad, they showed a

strong reluctance for channelling the funds directly back to
oil-importing developing countries. They rather preferred to
refer to commercial banks in industrial countries as an outlet
for investment. The international banking system reacted
promptly by accepting its role as financial intermediary
between major oil exporters and oil importers. Serving as a
clearing station included the task of transforming relatively
short-term capital brought in by OPEC to longer-term
credits required by Third World borrowers.

Although in 1977/78 the OPEC surplus was reduced,
liquidity of the Euromarket did not dry up. On the contrary,
market liquidity was further boosted bringing about a
borrowers' market (Fleming, 1981). The supply of funds was
fuelled by liquidity creating effects of soaring deficits in the
US trade balance and accompanying central bank interven-
tions in support of the US dollar. Unlike deficits in other
countries, which lead to a higher absorption of funds from
international capital markets, US deficits actually provided
additional funds because of the unique role of the US dollar
as a commonly held reserve currency (see, additionally,
Inoue, 1980).

The recycling of petro-dollars by commercial banks was
substantially alleviated by a number of innovations in
international financing techniques (Johnston, 1980). Mention may be made of the introduction of roll-over credits on
a large scale (i.e. issuing floating interest rates on bank
loans) and the development of syndicated loans. These new
techniques seemed well suited for improving risk sharing
among commercial banks. They permitted even smaller
creditors to participate in international lending which otherwise probably would have faced severe constraints in enter-
ing the market because of lack of experience and expertise.
The development of interbank markets in Eurocurrencies
facilitated the liability management of individual banks and
reduced their funding risk. It furthermore gave an impetus
to a stronger engagement of European and Far Eastern
commercial banks in international lending (see Fleming,
1981). Finally, formerly prevailing national restrictions to
capital exports were eased. This allowed, for example, an
expanded international engagement of Japanese banks in

1978 and 1979. Perhaps even more important was the removal of US capital controls in early 1974 (Llewellyn, 1979).

Accordingly, interbank competition was considerably strengthened just when the demand for credits in recession-hit industrial countries was rather weak. This may have induced a switching of funds by commercial banks from advanced to developing countries. The hypothesis of an inverse relationship between lending to industrial economies on the one hand and to NOPECs on the other may be supported by a comparison of growth rates calculated on the basis of banks' gross claims shown in Table 35. Actually, at times when the increase in banks' claims on all borrowers remained comparatively low (1974, 1975, 1980)[5] NOPECs' debt owed to banks mostly expanded very rapidly.[6] Moreover, high increases in overall market volumes went along with relatively small additional credits to NOPECs (1977 and 1978).[7] This evidence alone, however, is not very strong because fluctuations around the average growth rate of 24 per cent of banks' claims on all borrowers were rather limited (roughly 5 percentage points in both directions).[8]

The role of the demand for credits by industrial countries in determining the amount of funds channelled to NOPEC borrowers may be further analysed by referring to data on international bank loans as presented in Table 36. The observation that the amount of loans raised by OECD members was drastically reduced after 1974, whereas the provision of funds to NOPECs continued to rise, though at considerably retarded growth rates, can be stated in favour of the above-mentioned hypothesis. The same applies to 1979 when a slightly declining OECD demand went along with a remarkable increase in loans to NOPECs. Also, the year 1980 saw inverse developments: industrial countries reappeared on international capital markets and may have absorbed the major portion of available funds, thereby crowding out the NOPECs' demand for credits. On the other hand, both 1974 and 1978 were characterised by a notable parallel jump in credits raised by the two groups.[9]

A simple regression analysis casts further doubts on the general relevance of the hypothesis of an inverse relationship between lending to industrial and developing countries. The following regressions were run for the period 1973–80:[10]

$$LNO = a + b \cdot LOE + c \cdot T$$
$$\Delta LNO = a + b \cdot \Delta LOE$$

where:

LNO, LOE = international medium- and long-term bank loans raised by NOPECs and OECD countries, respectively

T = time trend

$\Delta LNO,$
ΔLOE = annual change in LNO and LOE.

In contrast to the expected negative signs of coefficients b in both equations the estimates remained insignificant. In the case of the first equation, the remarkably high adjusted R^2 (0.78) was only due to the trend variable T, which was highly significant with the expected positive sign. The computation of the second equation was completely skipped by the SPSS-programme applied, because of an insufficient F, or tolerance level. A control run replacing total NOPECs' lending by data for eighteen major borrowers resulted in an insignificant parameter value for $\triangle LOE$ together with an even negative adjusted R^2.

Although the results just presented probably are largely due to the very short period under consideration, it has to be concluded that the demand for credits in OECD member countries cannot explain international bank lending to NOPECs throughout the seventies. This does not rule out that, temporarily, a slackening demand by advanced borrowers induced an accelerated provision of loans to NOPECs. At other times, however, other factors seem to have overruled the impact of the OECD's demand for credits.

One of these other factors which deserve to be mentioned was the banks' desire to diversify their portfolios. Both the relaxation of capital controls in some industrial countries and the development of new financing techniques allowed a broadening of international bank activities. Many banks which previously were predominantly concerned with lend ing in domestic markets took the opportunity to spread risks internationally. This point has been elaborated by Johnston (1980, pp. 9–10):

If, in general, domestic economic activity and the risks of domestic borrower defaults are cyclical, so that the risks in lending to domestic borrowers are positively correlated, the scope for hedging risks in purely domestic loan portfolios will be limited. The risks in international lending, however, may appear to banks to be independent of domestic economic conditions. International loans provide banks with an enhanced range of investment opportunities—which allow the diversification of cyclical, sovereign and currency risks—and could provide banks with an attractive and effective means of increasing their lending activity and reducing overall portfolio risks.

A further, perhaps even more important incentive for banks to strengthen their international engagement was the relatively high return on offer in international capital markets at a time when the slackening loan demand in domestic markets threatened the deterioration of domestic profitability (Guth, 1981). Porzecanski (1981) presents estimates on the basis of financial statements of the ten internationally most active US banks, according to which the return on US domestic assets averaged 0.39 per cent in 1975, whereas the profit margin on international assets was 0.67 per cent. A similar picture prevailed in 1976, when profit margins of 0.40 per cent and 0.52 per cent, respectively, were calculated.[11] Although it is rather difficult to identify profitability in international lending to different country groups, the available evidence for US banks points to particularly high returns in lending to developing countries (O'Brien, 1981). According to World Bank data for the second half of the seventies (World Bank, Borrowing in International Capital Markets), average spreads above LIBOR on loans to developing economies (1.22 percentage points) exceeded spreads levied on industrial countries (0.87 percentage points) by 0.35 percentage points. In 1977 and 1978 the difference touched 0.5 percentage points. An analysis of banks' international earnings from individual US banks' balance sheets (Salomon Brothers, 1980; important findings summarised in

O'Brien, 1981) provides further support. Profitability on loans as measured by the spread between the yield on overseas loans and the rate paid on overseas interest-bearing deposits was found some 2 to 3 percentage higher in developing countries than in industrial countries.

Against the conclusion that lending to the Third World has clearly been attractive for banks in the seventies, it may be argued that comparatively favourable returns were just a reflection of higher risks attached to credits advanced to developing countries. However, besides the overall risk-spreading effects of the diversification in banks' portfolios mentioned above, the outcome of a survey of over 100 US banks carried out by Robert Morris Associates, asking respondents to identify the five borrowing countries where the largest international loan charge-offs were incurred, was rather favourable for Third World economies: aggregating total losses of banks under consideration for 1975–79, major NOPEC borrowers tended to have a proportionally (i.e. relative to banks' claims on them) lower loss record than, for example, Western European countries.[12]

Summing up, the expansion in bank lending to the Third World in the seventies seems to have been largely due to the fact that many NOPECs were regarded as good risks, promising bright profit chances. Economic disturbances after the first oil-price shock of 1973/74 were often regarded as only temporary. The negative impact of internationally retarding economic growth rates and other external shocks and problems arising from domestic policy failures in the Third World were understated, probably not only by borrowers but also by lenders. It is hard to blame only commercial banks for an assessment which later on proved to be a misconception. Up to the recent past, the banks' lending behaviour was praised by most observers as economically sound and well suited for guaranteeing a smooth recycling of petro-dollars. Moreover, as noted earlier, available indicator systems did not allow a safe prediction of future debt problems. Even in 1981, Solomon wrote (1982, p. 606; see also Blanchard, 1983):

The record of the major bank borrowers among developing

countries is favorable ... Mexico's oil and its prospects for continued rapid growth are strong elements in its creditworthiness. Brazil's export performance and its ability to compress imports provide a good deal of assurance about its capacity to prevent its external debt from becoming unmanageable even in the short run. In the longer run, the Brazilian 'miracle' should go on ...

Nevertheless, some questions remain open, casting doubts on the perception of banks' lending decisions as having been prudential and economically sound and later difficulties exclusively having arisen from developments which could not have been foreseen. First of all, it is surprising that the banks' credit engagement was heavily concentrated on developing countries which declared default later on (Noellert, 1979). The vast majority of banks' claims were held on Latin American borrowers (see Table 35). Only eight developing countries which were identified as the major problem borrowers within the sample of eighteen Third World economies—Argentina, Brazil, Chile, Mexico, Turkey, Venezuela, Yugoslavia and Zaire—accounted for 50 per cent of medium-term and long-term bank loans granted to all developing countries (OPEC countries included) in 1973–83 (Table 36). Even more astonishing, the share of the problem countries still increased in the more recent past, mounting from an average of 47 per cent in 1973–78 to 55 per cent in 1979–83. Because of this concentration, it is extremely dubious that 'the lack of structural uniformity of the countries within the OIDC [oil-importing developing country] category ensures that lending risk is well diversified' (Fleming, 1981, p. 31; see, additionally, Goodman, 1981).

Table 37 provides further evidence on the banks' unbalanced lending activities with respect to the Third World. As a percentage of US banks' capital, claims on all NOPECs averaged 130 per cent in 1977–82.[13] The ration was considerably higher for the nine largest US banks amounting to an average of 190 per cent. In both cases, the exposure to only Brazil and Mexico accounted for more than 40 per cent of figures for all NOPECs. Again, the banks' exposure to the most heavily indebted countries (as also to all NOPECs) still

Table 37: US Bank Lending to Non-Oil Developing Countries as Percent of Bank Capital, 1977–82

	1977	1978	1979	1980	1981	1982
All US Banks						
All NOPECs	114.9	114.4	124.2	132.3	148.3	146.1
Brazil and Mexico	56.8	52.0	50.3	53.0	61.2	63.4
Nine largest US banks						
All NOPECs	163.2	166.8	182.1	199.3	220.6	221.2
Brazil and Mexico	74.8	72.8	69.9	77.1	85.2	90.2
Selected US Banks[a]	Argentina	Brazil	Chile	Mexico	Venezuela	All five countries
Manufactures Hanover	47.5	77.7	28.4	66.7	42.4	262.8
Crocker National	38.1	57.3	26.5	51.2	22.8	196.0
Citibank	18.2	73.5	10.0	54.6	18.2	174.5
Chemical	14.9	52.0	14.8	60.0	28.0	169.7
Bank of America	10.2	47.9	6.3	52.1	41.7	158.2
Chase Manhattan	21.3	56.9	11.8	40.0	24.0	154.0
Bankers Trust	13.2	46.2	10.6	46.2	25.1	141.2
Morgan Guaranty	24.4	54.3	9.7	34.8	17.5	140.7

[a] End-1982.

Sources: Federal Reserve Board of Governors, *Country Exposure Lending Survey*; Prudential-Bache Securities, *Banking Industry Outlook*.

increased, comparing the late seventies and the early eighties. Taking five major Latin American problem borrowers together, the claims of selected US banks relative to their capital reached between 140 and 260 per cent in 1982. In many cases, loans to a single borrowing country exceeded half of the capital paid in.

Second, it is surprising that banks continued to lend to NOPECs on a large scale in the early eighties after the Third World has been hit by a new series of external shocks and domestic policy failures have become evident. This should have led to a correction of earlier misconceptions by banks. Though, compared to the seventies, growth rates in gross claims on all NOPECs have been reduced since 1980 (see Table 35), considerable amounts of fresh money were still channelled to NOPEC borrowers. For the problem-region Latin America, even the 1981 growth rate in gross debt owed to banks remained nearly unchanged (22.5 per cent against an average of 24.3 per cent in 1975–80). The amount of international medium-term and long-term bank loans raised by NOPECs in 1981 ($41.3 billion) was higher than ever before. Even in 1982 and 1983, total volumes of loans provided by banks considerably exceeded figures prevailing in the seventies (see Table 36), though it has to be taken into consideration that, especially in 1983, credits were largely absorbed for servicing maturing debt. It is furthermore noteworthy that the eight major problem borrowers also succeeded in obtaining huge amounts of loans in the early eighties.

The fact that in mid-1982 new lending to NOPECs (net of repayments) was drastically stopped by banks is commonly regarded as a dramatic shift in banks' policies towards the Third World.[14] Especially for Latin America, net lending was practically nil in the second half of 1982, against $11.7 billion in the six months before. According to estimates of the World Bank, the traditional direction of net transfers (i.e. gross lending minus repayment and minus interest payments) from developed to developing countries with respect to medium-term and long-term debt from private sources was reversed recently. In 1983 developing countries experienced net capital outflows of $21 billion against positive net transfers of $16 billion in 1981 (*Neue Zürcher Zeitung*, 11 February 1984; see also Clausen, 1983).

Undoubtedly, the acute Mexican debt crisis in mid-1982 marked a milestone in banks' lending policies to developing countries. Reconsidering their exposure to Third World borrowers, many banks decided to cut the expansion of their credit engagement drastically. But why, it may be asked, didn't they try harder to *reduce* their engagements? With the exception of smaller banks which sometimes aimed at withdrawing funds from debt-problem-ridden developing countries, most private lenders agreed in providing new funds in order to enable borrowers to service old debt. Frequently, not only debt repayment was postponed by rescheduling programmes (which would have left the banks' exposure unchanged) but also additional funds were granted in order to finance interest payments falling due which further aggravated the banks' exposure.

One may argue that banks tried to gain time, instead of withdrawing funds as far as possible, because they continually believed that the repayment difficulties of borrowers were rather short-term. Moreover, their lending in the most recent past may at least partly be called 'involuntary' (Cline, 1983, pp. 73–8). Borrowers pressed banks already highly exposed to them to provide new money by stating that otherwise they may be forced to repudiate their debt owed to banks. Accordingly, banks which wanted to avoid an immediate realisation of losses were in a lender's trap. Pressures were also exerted by official creditors, especially the IMF, which sometimes made their financial engagement in rescue operations conditional on a further increase in bank's exposure.

Economically, throwing good money after the bad made only sense if debt difficulties were likely to be overcome in the near future. This, however, was hardly to be expected. Prospects for a significant improvement in international economic conditions remained remote (for a more detailed discussion, see Ch. 11). Attempts of borrowers to reshape domestic economic policies in order to correct previous policy failures would probably need a good deal of time to become effective, if such attempts were undertaken at all. Thus it could not have been very surprising to banks that most rescue operations proved to be short-winded. In several cases payment difficulties reappeared at the surface only shortly afterwards.

That is why on both counts—the heavy concentration on problem debtors and the continued provision of capital in the recent past—the perception of banks' policies towards the Third World as having been economically sound may be questioned (Williams *et al.*, 1982, p. 8; see also Pöhl, 1981, p. 29). Against this background it seems justified to consider factors which may have induced lending decisions which were imprudent at least from a global economic viewpoint, if not in the banks' own perception. The most critical point to be raised is the question of whether risks really were not foreseeable or whether risks were rather disregarded and, under given circumstances, perhaps even did not need to be properly analysed by banks. In the latter case, bank lending might have been beyond the 'maximum safe level of borrowing' (Eaton, Gersovitz, 1981a, p. 290) at which the borrowers' costs just exceed their benefits of default (see also Eaton, Gersovitz, 1981b; Sachs, Cohen, 1982).

A discounting of risks may already be due to internal bureaucratic decision-making of commercial banks. Similar to public administrations, where heads of different departments are supposed to strive for improving their personal status by artificially raising the demand for goods or services supplied by them,[15] bank division chiefs and loan-marketing officers may aim at maximising loan approvals to the country or region they are concerned with because annual bonuses and career prospects are at stake (Palmer, *et al.*, 1983). Accordingly, they will stress aspects which may be put in favour of lending and suppress objections to it (Glismann, Nunnenkamp, 1983). If the credit fails later on, the responsibility may be given to 'unforeseeable' events or factors 'outside the bank's control'. Moreover, meanwhile the man who took the decision might have changed to another position in many cases.

Turning to the syndication of credits, the principally positive risk sharing between different banks achieved in this way is only one face of the coin. The dark side may be a cumulation of faults. The unbalanced bank lending to Latin America, for example, was probably fostered by largely ruling out independent decision-making of individual creditors. Especially smaller banks were likely to rely heavily on the judgements of the major banks arranging syndications (see also de Grauwe, Fratianni, 1983). This kind of cartelisation strongly impeded individual creditors from striving against the current; this could have reduced the concentration of risks on specific borrowers or regions.

Furthermore, risks attached to external financing of specific projects in developing countries may be frequently neglected by banks which felt safeguarded against losses because the bulk of credits was raised by governments, or at least officially guaranteed. In the case of failing projects, the banks assumed that the state would pick up the bill. Accordingly, in lending to developing countries the banks' control of how their money was used seemed often less strict than in lending to domestic corporate borrowers (see Beloff, 1983; Greiff, Martin, 1981). Similarly, trade related credits provided by banks often carried guarantees of the exporting countries' governments so that banks didn't need to bother about risks.

Even if the creditors' confidence that borrowing countries' guarantees would secure the repayment of loans proved to be illusive, as it did in the recent past, there was a second line of defence against significant losses possibly arising from lending to the Third World. As soon as the necessary write-offs due to borrowers' defaults began to threaten the economic well-being of creditor banks, it could be assumed that official rescue measures would be adopted. According to a widespread view, banks should be officially bailed out in a critical situation in order to prevent overall economic conditions from being negatively affected. The reliance on domestic central banks and international organisations like the IMF, which were supposed to step in as lenders of last resort if commercial banks would run into troubles, is likely to have further reduced the risk-consciousness of private lenders (Sjaastad, 1983, pp. 310–11).

Experiences of the early eighties strongly confirmed the banks' belief in official support in the case of developing countries facing major difficulties in servicing their bank debt. Actually, the Bank for International Settlements, acting on behalf of the central banks of the Group of Ten countries, provided bridging finance in several instances. The IMF arranged many rescheduling programmes and made considerable amounts of official credits available to debt-problem-ridden developing countries. Although official lending was sometimes made conditional on further loans provided by private debtors, it seems likely that IMF and related official activities were welcomed by banks because they got a chance to transfer their own risks at least partly to official agencies. The supposition that banks aim at socialising private losses was stressed again by their support of an increase in IMF quotas recently agreed upon, which should further raise the IMF's potential to lend. Other proposals presently discussed to alleviate the critical debt situation would probably also result in shifting the burden to the public (for a more detailed discussion, see Ch. 12). Therefore, the continued bank lending to already over-indebted Third World countries in the past may be attributed to moral hazard rather than to persistent hopes of only temporary repayment difficulties of borrowers. It seems plausible to argue that banks heavily engaged in problem countries are interested in improving, in the meantime, both material and intellectual conditions for a socialisation of losses (Meltzer, 1983). In other words the argument of gaining time may have two completely different meanings.

NOTES

1. For a detailed description of different concepts of the Eurocurrency market, *see* Dennis, 1983; for the BIS procedure of netting out interbank transactions, *see*, additionally, Mayer, 1976 and Johnston, 1983.
2. The expression 'net' in this context should be distinguished from banks' net claims on countries as presented in Table 35, where banks' liabilities to countries are subtracted from gross claims.
3. The net liabilities of Eastern Europe to commercial banks were highest in 1981, when they amounted to $46 billion (BIS, Inter-

national Banking Developments). Both developed economies within the reporting area and OPEC member countries were net suppliers of funds to the Euromarket.

4. Sometimes the share of Latin America in banks' net assets vis-à-vis all NOPECs exceeded 100 per cent. This was largely due to NOPECs located in the Middle East (not separately stated in Table 35). They continuously provided net funds to the Euromarket. In the mid-seventies Asia and Africa temporarily were also net suppliers.

5. The annual average increase in banks' total claims in 1973–80 stood at 23.8 per cent. At the beginning of this period, growth rates of 22 per cent (1974) and 22.4 per cent (1975) were calculated. The figure for 1980 was 19 per cent.

6. Compared to the average increase of 29.3 per cent in NOPECs' liabilities to banks in 1973–80, growth rates were particularly high in 1974 (46.9 per cent) and 1975 (34 per cent). In 1980, however, the increase in liabilities to banks was below the respective averages for both NOPECs (24.1 per cent) and all borrowers (19 per cent).

7. Total market volumes expanded by 26 per cent (1977) and 29.5 per cent (1978). The respective growth rates for NOPEC borrowers amounted to 20.1 per cent and 23.4 per cent.

8. Of course, it would make more sense to compare NOPEC figures to bank lending within the reporting area of industrial countries only, than to overall market volumes. Fluctuations in annual growth rates were by far greater for the reporting area's liabilities, ranging from 14.6 to 33.6 per cent. Separate data for this country group have been available only since 1975, however. Therefore, overall market volumes were taken as a reference measure.

9. The fact that inverse and parallel developments, respectively, did not occur in the same years with respect to international bank loans on the one hand and to growth in banks' total claims outstanding on the other, is probably due to a whole set of factors. First, it has to be recalled that in the latter case, NOPECs are not compared to industrial borrowers only but to overall market volumes which include a considerable amount of double-counting because of inter-bank lending. Second, differences are likely to result from the exclusion of short-term loans in Table 36. Additionally, the banks' claims as presented in Table 35 are reduced by repayments of borrowers on maturing loans, whereas data on new international bank loans disregard repayments.

10. The years 1981–83 were left out of account because with debt-servicing problems of NOPECs becoming obvious, it was no longer to be expected that the demand for credits in industrial countries would significantly influence the amount of funds channelled to NOPECs.

11. In 1979 the situation had changed, however. The return on US domestic assets had improved considerably to 0.57 per cent and the margin on international assets has been squeezed to 0.44 per cent.

12. For a presentation of the main findings of the study, *see* Porzecanski, 1981. Of course, the survey remains only tentative in portraying risks

attached to international lending to different country groups. Losses incurred in many smaller developing countries were probably of insufficient size to be included among the top five countries. Moreover, it seems that banks' write-off decisions were especially complicated in the case of Third World countries. Often the major share of credits was raised by official borrowers, which could hardly be forced by foreign banks to liquidate their assets when difficulties in debt servicing emerged. Consequently, banks sometimes agreed on rescheduling or debt relief, which may have affected the quality of banks' portfolios and their risk perception but which is not apparent from data on loss records.

13. For information on UK banks, *see* Johnson, 1983, p. 11; for most other industrial countries, similar information is not available (*see* Williams *et al.*, 1982, pp. 43–3).

14. For a presentation and interpretation of half-annually data, *see* BIS, *International Banking Developments*, Second Quarter 1983; whereas in the first half of 1982, funds raised by all NOPECS still exceeded their repayments by \$15.4 billion, net flows dropped to \$4.7 billion in the second half of 1982, with only a slight improvement to \$5.8 billion in the first six months of 1983.

15. For an elaboration of a theory of bureaucracy, *see*, for example, Buchanan, 1978; Niskanen, 1971; Rowley, 1979.

Part III
POSSIBLE CONSEQUENCES

8 The Thirties and the Eighties: A Comparison

Until recently the international indebtedness of developing countries was largely ignored by most politicians and the press. Only specialised circles, for example those focusing on North–South relations, discussed questions arising from the Third World's foreign debt. Even here, however, the perspective remained rather narrow. A major fraction of developing countries advocated official debt relief provided by lenders' governments because high and rising debt-service payments were regarded as detrimental to further growth and industrialisation prospects (see Wionczek *et al.*, 1978, pp. 98–118; Navarrete, 1978). In the industrialised world hardly anyone was interested in these discussions, except the finance ministers fighting against further claims on their already distressed budgets.

Only in the very recent past, when an increasing number of borrowers failed to meet their debt-service obligations, the situation changed drastically. The international debt situation suddenly became a prominent issue of public debate, as it was understood that debt problems are not restricted to borrowers but may rather produce major drawbacks for the economic well-being of lending nations too. In sharp contrast to the formerly prevailing careless treatment of foreign indebtedness of developing countries— and of Eastern Bloc nations—it was now the time of doomsday scenarios. According to them, defaults of some of the Third World's biggest borrowers would trigger the collapse of the whole international financial system, which, as a corollary, would sharply reduce international trade and production, the final consequence being a worldwide depression comparable to the Great Depression of the twenties and thirties. Here is just one example of the hectic nervousness since mid-1982. On the occasion of the 1982 meetings

113

of the IMF and the World Bank in Toronto, Denis Healey, the former British Chancellor of the Exchequer stated that 'the risk of a major default triggering a chain reaction is growing every day' (*New York Times*, 12 September 1982). He regarded the Toronto meetings as 'the last chance to save the world from a catastrophe even greater than the slump of the 1930s'.

Since then the mood of panic has cooled somewhat. Lenders' governments, private banks and international institutions like the IMF adopted quick rescue packages which not only enabled developing countries in payment troubles to reschedule maturing credits but also provided them with additional funds. It cannot be denied that emergency programmes launched by the international financial community have so far been successful in sparing commercial banks unmanageably large write-offs of poor loans, thereby interrupting the course of the doomsday scenarios right at the beginning. However, as new and continued repayment difficulties of Third World countries showed, these measures proved to be rather short-winded (for a more detailed discussion of rescheduling practices, see Ch. 10). Moreover, World Bank officials predicted that reschedulings agreed upon in the past will lead to an alarming bunching of maturities in 1986/87 (*Frankfurter Allgemeine Zeitung*, 1 March 1984), which again may highlight what would be at stake for the economic well-being of both debtor and creditor nations in the event of major defaults. It therefore seems highly desirable to thoroughly review the relevance of doomsday scenarios and the likelihood of another Great Depression.

Before turning in Chapter 9 to an analysis of chain reactions possibly called forth by widespread debt problems of Third World borrowers, the remaining part of this chapter is devoted to a short comparison of the economic conditions prevailing in the twenties and thirties on the one hand and in the early eighties on the other hand. This presentation will help in an assessment of whether the Great Depression is really a relevant period to be referred to in view of present economic tensions, or whether the perception of the Third World's repayment problems as a factor which may break the camel's back is mere scaremongering. The latter cannot be ruled out altogether, since it has been shown above that commercial banks may be heavily interested in improving the climate for a socialisation of losses. Accordingly, the dissemination of the nightmare of an economic catastrophe arising from failures of banks which are highly exposed in the Third World may make the public much more inclined to take over banks' private losses.

Reviewing the literature on the causes of the Great Depression of the thirties, one comes up with a whole bundle of factors which may explain the worldwide slump (Ahnefeld *et al.*, 1982, p. 8).[1] While the relative importance of individual factors is highly controversial, many observers agree that a chain of events, simultaneously occurring and reinforcing each other, finally resulted in the Depression. At least partly, the crisis may be traced back to distortions which already emerged in earlier times. Frequently, increases in real wages exceeded the amount which was compatible with maintaining high employment levels. In most countries economic policies were rather volatile. Unforeseeable changes in orientation made private economic agents' calculations subject to considerable risks. Governments in many respects intervened in the market mechanism, thereby impeding and postponing structural adjustments for the sake of short-sighted employment considerations.[2]

The fact that misallocations accumulated in the past broke forth in a severe depression can be largely attributed to procyclical policies of both governments and central banks (Glismann, Rodemer, 1982, p. 6). Confronted with declining tax revenues, governments reduced their spending rather than allowing for credit-financed budget deficits. Central banks failed in compensating for the private economic agents' increased preference in holding money by maintaining the expansion of the money base. In the United States, for example, the broad money supply (M2) decreased by more than a third from August 1929 to March 1933 (Vaubel, 1984). This unprecedented contraction seems to have been the decisive reason for the severity of the Depression (see, additionally, Friedman, Schwartz, 1967).

Policy mistakes resulted in the collapse of many firms and in widespread bank failures. More than one-fifth of all US commercial banks representing nearly one-tenth of total deposits suspended operations from August 1929 to March 1933. In Germany the whole banking system collapsed temporarily in July 1931 (Vaubel, 1984).

Those who argue that current economic tensions may erupt in another Great Depression state that the situation in the early eighties is similar to the one that led to the slump in the thirties. In fact, the number of firms experiencing payment difficulties has soared dramatically. Bankruptcy figures reached levels never previously observed in the last three decades. This has caused concern about the liquidity position of commercial banks, which already were subject to difficulties arising from international lending, both to developing countries and Eastern Bloc nations. Although major bank failures have not occurred up to now, many observers consider the banking system to be considerably weakened.

Summarising the analogy between underlying factors, Vaubel (1984) comes up with a rather long list of similarities between the recent past and the years preceding the Great Depression. In both instances:

1. The decline in real income may be attributed to restrictive US monetary policies.
2. Real interest rates have been extraordinarily high.
3. Real disturbances and maladjustments may have added to the decline in real income.
4. The reduction in real income was associated with spreading protectionism.
5. The US dollar strengthened, US terms-of-trade improved and the US capital-account balance increased.
6. Foreign lending was part of an international recycling process.[3]
7. Foreign debtors suspended debt service and creditor countries granted official emergency loans.
8. US economic policies are widely blamed for economic tensions in other countries.
9. A lack of international coordination of economic policies is widely claimed to have aggravated economic difficulties.

Although some of these similarities may be merely super-ficial, others deserve further consideration. As in the case of the Great Depression, present economic problems are probably largely due to earlier developments. Since the late sixties, governments increasingly took the stance that they have to be the driving force of economic growth. In a Keynesian mood, policy-makers shifted towards expansion-ary monetary and fiscal policies in order to accelerate the establishment of the modern welfare state (Giersch, 1982). Full employment was officially guaranteed without consider-ing consequences arising from this shift in responsibilities. Trade unions no longer needed to consider negative employ-ment effects of unsuitably high wage increases. Conse-quently, the bargaining behaviour of trade unions became more aggressive, which drove real wages beyond levels compatible with full employment under pure market con-ditions.

The distributional struggles between the public and the private sector on the one hand and, within the private sector, between capital and labour on the other hand can be considered to have notably contributed to severe mis-allocations of scarce resources. To the extent that govern-ments used acquired funds for consumptive purposes and more productive private projects were crowded out, econ-omic growth prospects were eroded. Distortions in rela-tive factor prices—that is, excessively high labour costs and an artificially depressed price of capital—favoured 'a mode of thinking directed towards short-term achieve-ments rather than long-term planning, towards distributing what has not yet been produced, and towards burdening the economy with commitments for the present rather than making it weatherproof for the future' (Giersch, 1982, p. 205).

The role of distributional struggles in worsening con-ditions for economic growth is stressed by analyses of long waves in economic development. Rising government expen-diture shares in GDP are supposed to reduce incentives for both entrepreneurs and employees to individually strive for an improvement in their living standards. Both the economic crisis in the thirties and economic tensions in the recent past were accompanied by high and rising government consumption shares (Glismann, Rodemer, Wolter, 1983, pp. 153–5). With respect to the real wage position, again a mirror image emerged when comparing the cyclical pattern of wages with the cycles in investment activity and national product. The results suggest that 'at least during the period from 1925 to the present, wages were a decisive determinant of profit developments and thereby contributed to the emergence and course of investment and growth cycles' (Glismann, Rodemer, Wolter, 1983, p. 156).

As in the thirties, the negative effects of structural distortions on economic growth and employment levels—effects which accumulated in the seventies—came to be felt only after some delay. Temporarily, economic growth and full employment could be achieved at the expense of an accelerating inflation. But 'inflation stimulates demand and growth only if it comes *unexpectedly* and is not anticipated in wage contracts and interest rates' (Giersch, 1982, p. 205). When the rate of inflation went beyond its tolerable level and money-illusion could no longer be exploited, the damage of former policy failures became obvious. In the meantime, however, the costs of adjustment had increased considerably because of accumulated misallocations and deep-rooted inflationary expectations. That is why the medicine prescribed for economic recovery had to be rather painful.

Similar to the late twenties and early thirties, the medicine consisted mainly of restrictive monetary policies. In the United States the rate of change in broad money supply (M2) declined by 3.5 percentage points in the period from the end of 1980 to mid-1982. This restriction, however, was rather modest compared to the sharp contraction of M2 fifty years ago. It merely resulted in a slower expansion of the money supply. Consequently, US consumer prices continued to rise in the early eighties, while the price level fell by almost a quarter from 1929 to 1933 (Vaubel, 1984). Nevertheless, a striking analogy existed between both periods: with respect to the annual rates of change in consumer prices, a decline of slightly more than 10 percentage points within three years was to be observed in both cases.[4]

Disinflationary policies of the recent past caused real interest rates to soar to dramatically high levels. A large proportion of investments was based on extremely low or even negative real rates of interest prevailing in the seventies and had to be written off. Moreover, the shock therapy triggered considerable output and employment losses, which, as a corollary, strengthened the protectionist sentiment. Just as in the thirties, government measures likely to aggravate recessionary tendencies accumulated when economic difficulties broke forth.[5] As Glismann, Rodemer and Wolter wrote (1983, p. 153), generally speaking:

If, through rising unemployment, the public becomes generally aware of an enduring deterioration of the economic situation, the conviction that additional protective measures are an appropriate antidote to the crisis gains ground. During the 1920s and early 1930s this view led to international competition in protectionism, which substantially accelerated the economic decline. At present, too, in numerous Western countries—particularly in the countries of the European Community—the belief that national economic difficulties can be overcome by additional protection is gaining ground.

To many observers it seems that these beggar-my-neighbour policies considerably contributed to the Great Depression (see Arndt, 1944, p. 295; Kindleberger, 1973, pp. 292, 295). Accordingly, a lack of international policy coordination is also considered to be a present danger, which may cause the poor economic performance of the early eighties to deteriorate further (Kindleberger, 1978, p. 226). This certainly holds true with respect to the trade policies I have just mentioned, where international agreements should aim at averting worldwide competition in protectionism. In other respects, however, the situation is different, especially in the field of monetary policies. Both in the thirties and in the recent past, too much rather than too little international collusion could be observed (Vaubel, 1984; Ahnefeld *et al.*, 1982, p. 8). Fifty years ago adherence to the gold standard led to an automatic international transmission of policy failures in the United States. Today the widely held preference for fixed or at least less flexible

exchange rates contributes to an international synchronis-
ation of economic developments. The concertation of
national policies is likely to further enhance economic
tensions on an international scale.[6]

Summing up the short review of economic conditions and
underlying factors prevailing half a century ago on the one
hand and in the recent past on the other, striking similarities
cannot be denied. Nevertheless, it should not be too difficult
to prevent another Great Depression in the eighties. Monetary authorities can avoid liquidity crises (and probable chain
reactions) by compensating for an eventual increase in
liquidity preferences of the public. Governments can resist
protectionist pressures, thereby supporting a continuous
growth in international trade.

On the other hand, there is some reason for pessimism.
The strengthening of protectionist sentiments in recent years
seems to indicate that policy-makers have not learnt their
lessons. Moreover, the ability of governments to solve
current economic problems is widely questioned. Though
the demand-orientated Keynesian approach has largely
failed, a re-orientation of economic policies is frequently still
resisted. The further delay in adjustment, however, gives
rise to a widespread mistrust in public authorities. This is
why another Great Depression cannot be ruled out altogether. Consequently, a more specific evaluation of possible
international drawbacks of developing countries' defaults
seems in place.

NOTES

1. As a more recent example, *see* Brunner, 1981.
2. These and other longer-run structural influences are stressed, for
    example, in Arndt, 1944, pp. 276 ff. and Haberler, 1976, pp. 22–30.
3. In the twenties and thirties the Germans were obliged to pay
    reparations to European nations. These countries, in turn, had to
    repay their war debt to the United States, which rechannelled funds
    back to Germany. In the recent past, commercial banks in indus-
    trialised countries recycled OPEC's petro-dollars to NOPECs.
4. Fifty years ago the rate of change in US consumer prices declined

from 0.0 per cent in 1928/29 to −10.3 per cent in 1931/32; recently, figures declined from 13.5 per cent in 1979/80 to 3.2 per cent in 1982/83.

5.   For the thirties, *see* Kindleberger, 1973; for the recent past, *see* inventories prepared by the General Agreement on Tariffs and Trade (GATT), IMF and UNCTAD.

6.   For a detailed critique of international coordination of national macro-economic policies, *see* Vaubel, 1983a.

9 Possible International Impact of Borrowing Countries' Defaults

Among the analogies which can be observed between the thirties and the eighties, one that figures prominently is the borrowers' difficulty in servicing their foreign loans. At the end of 1935 nearly 40 per cent of all foreign bonds traded on the New York Stock Exchange had ceased to be serviced. This applied not only to nearly all German bonds but also to 80 per cent of Latin American bonds (Vaubel, 1984). Some countries even repudiated their debt (for further details, see Madden *et al.*, 1937, pp. 111–25; Díaz Alejandro, 1983). Similarly, the early eighties experienced a sharp increase in the numbers of borrowers with debt difficulties who asked for rescheduling. In the seventies an annual average number of only two to three countries rescheduled an aggregate annual average amount of $1.3 billion in foreign debt (Anderson, 1982). Later on, figures jumped to fourteen borrowers asking for $11 billion in 1981, followed by more than twenty borrowers and $40 billion (according to preliminary data) in 1982 (see, additionally, *Frankfurter Allgemeine Zeitung*, 10 September 1982). The amount of $40 billion in 1982 considerably exceeded the aggregated total which was rescheduled in the last twenty-five years. Moreover, external payments arrears incurred by IMF member countries have risen sharply since the late seventies, reaching $7.2 billion in 1981 (IMF, *Annual Report on Exchange Arrangements and Exchange Restrictions*). The number of countries reporting arrears more than doubled from 1975 to 1981, from fifteen to thirty-five. In 1982, arrears further dramatically gained in importance, soaring to nearly $15 billion, while the number of countries concerned remained constant. Increasingly, relatively advanced economies in Latin America and Eastern Europe also accumulated arrears.

As the banking system collapsed in the thirties, some

observers fear that this can happen again. The vulnerability of the banking system stems from the fact that credits which were extended to foreign borrowers and which are now at risk amount to a large portion of the banks' capital. It has been estimated that about two-thirds of the banks' total claims on Eastern Europe and the Third World can be considered as bad loans because of recent interruptions in debt servicing (Cline, 1983, pp. 32–6). At the end of 1981 liabilities of the eight problem countries (identified in Ch. 4) to private banks in the BIS reporting area stood at 56 per cent of the banks' capital.[1] The situation is critical in particular for some major US banks which are highly exposed to Latin American problem borrowers (see Table 37, p. 102). More than 90 per cent of the capital base of the nine largest US banks would be wiped out if just Brazil and Mexico completely defaulted on their foreign debt. For certain banks the threat of losses fully absorbing paid-in capital is even greater. In the case of Manufactures Hanover, for example, Mexico's liabilities alone amounted to 67 per cent of capital; loans given to five Latin American problem borrowers exceeded the capital base by more than 160 per cent.

In contrast to the thirties, when the creditors were mainly individual bondholders, today mainly the commercial banks in industrial countries will be adversely affected by developing countries' defaults. The probability of bank failures, however, not only depends on the level of loan/capital ratios reached but, and most important, on the incentives for borrowers to default and the treatment of defaulted loans by bank regulators in the creditor countries. Turning first to the latter point, it has to be stressed that the impact of defaults on the financial position of creditor banks is subject to write-off regulations. A prescription requiring an immediate write-off of non-performing loans to zero would be most likely to force banks to close. Such a prescription, however, seems neither necessary nor desirable (Weintraub, 1983a, pp. 21, 29). First of all, there may still be a market value above zero for the loans, because defaults are perceived not as permanent and there is hope for a correction of the borrower's decision to default. But even if there are no reasonable prospects for debt servicing later on, financial strains for banks facing losses may be substantially eased. Banks may be allowed time to stretch loan losses over several years. A smooth adjustment will be alleviated if expected profits, arising from domestic operations for example, may be used to compensate for losses in international lending. Given time, banks may succeed in broadening their capital base, thereby improving the capacity to absorb losses without affecting further operations. The possibilities of preventing bank failures by liberal write-off regulations remain remote, however, in cases of very heavy losses. The banks' depositors will refuse to provide fresh capital if they expect that this would increase the amount of money lost rather than help a smooth adjustment.

With respect to the borrowers' incentives to default, the following difference between the thirties and the recent past seems important. While formerly a large part of the European foreign debt was owed by private enterprises and banks, today's debtors are mainly public authorities, either directly or indirectly because of governments' guarantees attached to private loans. Accordingly, Vaubel (1984, pp. 9–10) writes:

the bargaining position of foreign debtors is now incomparably stronger than it was in the thirties: by threatening complete default on their foreign debt, the *sovereign* debtors of banks do not lose their borrowing potential at home *and* can play with the menace of bank failures and monetary disruptions in the creditor countries. There is evidence that the governments of the debtor countries are fully aware of the threat potential which they have at their disposal, especially if they combine to form a debtors' cartel.

The incentives for borrowers to declare default are frequently considered rather weak. This is based on the assumption that countries which unilaterally cease to service foreign loans or even repudiate their debt, would not be able to raise new loans indefinitely. But even if it is accepted that credit sources would dry up altogether, complete defaults cannot be ruled out. First of all, borrowers will not decide on purely economic grounds. In fact, economic considerations may play only a secondary role, particularly in the case of politically unstable regimes. It may be that public pressures urging the 'punishment' of foreign creditors which are perceived as exploiting the borrowing country can no longer be resisted.

Even in purely economic terms, however, the cost/benefit ratio of potential default has probably deteriorated in the recent past (see Eaton, Gersovitz, 1981a; 1981b; Sachs, Cohen, 1982). With the rising amount of accumulated debt, potential benefits have increased. On the other hand, the reluctance of creditors to provide fresh money has reduced the potential costs of default. Autarchic sentiments on the borrowers' side may have been further strengthened by the mounting protectionism of industrial countries, which blocks an economically sound way of alleviating the debt burden. It therefore seems reasonable to conclude that the probability of defaults has increased rather than decreased. Notwithstanding liberal write-off regulations, some banks may then be forced to close if loan losses become unmanageably high.

In discussing the possible consequences of bank failures one may refer to 'the near crisis of 1974' (Johnson, 1983, pp. 9, 13). Although the bank failures of 1974—the most important of which were Franklin National Bank and Bankhaus Herstatt—were not triggered by defaults of Third World borrowers, they can give some indication of the potential difficulties and ramifications. The failures led many banks to withdraw from international banking, at least temporarily. Other banks experienced considerable funding problems because large money-centre banks drastically reduced the placement of funds and increasingly discriminated between net takers in the interbank market. Consequently, commitments dropped abruptly; from 1974 to 1975, the volume of international lending was squeezed by about 20 per cent. The terms of remaining commitments hardened sharply. Maturities of loans were significantly lowered, from an average of eight years to about five years. Average spreads charged by banks for intermediary services more than doubled, exceeding 1.5 per cent.

That international drawbacks of financial strains in 1974 remained manageable may be largely attributed to fortunate circumstances prevailing in the mid-seventies. Because of

the recession in most industrial countries their demand for
international bank credit was rather weak. Otherwise, developing countries would probably have faced substantially
stronger and prolonged difficulties in obtaining fresh money
from international capital markets. Since similar lucky
chances cannot be relied upon in the future, the costs and
consequences of recurring strains in the capacity and willingness of international banks to intermediate may be much
higher and more severe.

According to some observers, presently a serious danger
exists that difficulties of individual banks will spread quickly
from one bank to another because of strong interbank
connections (see the quotations in Weintraub, 1983a, pp.
24–5). The following scenario examplifies some typical
misgivings (*The Wall Street Journal*, 10 November 1982).
The starting point of the crisis scenario presented is the
bankruptcy of a rather small lending company. Shortly
afterwards, a bank that specialises on intermediation
between big money-centre banks and small companies like
the one that failed experiences severe funding problems.
The depositors of another bank, which is responsible for
bailing out the sister company become worried and shift
their deposits elsewhere. Huge sums of money begin to
move. Groups of banks in places considered less safe
become shaky. Banks that are perceived to be in trouble run
out of funds. Debt repudiation or default is conceived as the
key event: when an important Latin American borrower
repudiates its external debt, banks begin to fall like nine-
pins. The collapse of the whole financial system then triggers
a marked decline in international trade. Enterprises close,
unemployment levels soar, and the final result is depression.

Is this scenario mere panic-stirring or can it be regarded as
a realistic presentation of probable chain reactions? Given
the possibility of some bank failures, an analysis of further
complications has to consider different modes of reactions of
economic agents involved. First, it has to be stressed that
unless there is a general liquidity crisis an individual bank
cannot face a liquidity problem (Vaubel, 1984). In other
words, if a bank fails in maintaining operations by selling
long-term assets in order to improve its liquidity, this is a

case of insolvency.[2] In the past, bank insolvencies have been typically dealt with by merger. The absorption of bankrupt concerns by sound and larger banks has tended to guarantee all deposits of the failing bank's creditors (Cline, 1983, p. 39). In this way, further complications could be largely avoided. The fact, however, that today's risks of failures are mainly concentrated on the largest banks may render this solution more difficult in future. In the event of insolvency, no bank may exist which is strong enough to absorb the whole insolvent concern. Consequently, the probability has increased that at least a fraction of deposits of the failing bank's creditors will be lost, namely those not covered by depositors' insurance systems. For the United States, for example, only about 75 per cent of total deposits would be guaranteed by the Federal Depositors' Insurance Corporation, as the coverage is restricted to $100 000 per account.

The depositors' risks of losing money in the event of bank failures will induce them to react quickly if they consider their bank to be in trouble. Depositors will try to withdraw their funds as far as possible. This attempt will be at least partly successful, since most external liabilities of banks typically have relatively short maturities compared to their assets (Guttentag, Herring, 1983, p.6). Worried depositors may demand payment on their checkable deposits, saving accounts and maturing time deposits (Weintraub, 1983a, pp. 27–8). A few large depositors, who may be relatively well informed about the bank's financial position, reacting in this way are likely to trigger a process of contagion resulting in a general run on the bank concerned.

Such withdrawals will not affect the banking system as a whole, however, if the depositors' mistrust is limited to an individual bank or certain banks only; for example, those holding the major share of loans formerly extended to developing countries and now threatened by their default. In this case, only these banks will probably encounter mounting difficulties. In attempting to meet depositors' requests, they 'need to substitute new liabilities for those being run off or to carry out a parallel runoff of assets. The cost of doing so rises sharply with the volume of funds that the banks attempt to acquire, severely constraining their ability to make new loans and, ultimately, threatening bank solvency' (Johnson, 1983, p. 12).

The system's consolidated accounts would not be affected at all by transferring deposits from a bank perceived as financially strained to another bank regarded as a sound address. In such a zero-sum switch some banks will gain what others will lose. This also holds true if withdrawn deposits leave the banking system initially; for example, through depositors using the funds for payments to non-bank third parties. Whether payments are made 'to purchase stocks, bonds, goods and services, or to pay-down debts, payees' banks would gain the reserves and, directly or as a corollary, the deposits that payers' banks had lost' (Weintraub, 1983a, p. 27).

Only a *general* mistrust of the public in the banking system's ability to cope with losses arising from developing countries' defaults can trigger the severe worldwide drawbacks inherent in doomsday scenarios like the one presented above. If depositors fear that they will lose their deposits, irrespective of where they are placed, a simultaneous run on banks will set in. The funds withdrawn will not be transferred to other banks, either by former depositors or by non-bank third parties carrying out transactions with former depositors. Funds will rather be retained and hoarded by the public.

Under these circumstances, all banks would be in need to substitute new liabilities for those withdrawn. They cannot succeed, however. The characteristics of the interbank market will rather cause a quick transmission of funding problems (Johnson, 1983, pp. 12–13). The widespread withdrawal of deposits by the public will, first of all, hit the relatively small number of large banks which traditionally were favoured by most important depositors as outlets for their funds. The chances of these banks replacing lost deposits will be remote because they themselves formerly were the net suppliers of capital in interbank markets. They will not be able to perform their role any longer and will rather be forced to insist on collecting funds due to them from other banks. This will cause a serious liquidity drain for net takers in interbank markets; that is, for those banks which traditionally relied heavily on large money-centre banks for net funding. In other words, international financial intermediation will be disrupted and interbank markets will dry up quickly in case of a general run on banks.

Faced by a general liquidity crisis, banks will be forced to cut down their claims accordingly in order to restore balance-sheet ratios required by bank regulators. In the United States, for example, a formal requirement of 5 per cent capital backing of loans has been adopted (Cline, 1983, p. 38). That is to say, if banks' losses due to non-performing loans affect their capital base, this will induce a twenty-fold reduction in loan provisions, provided the potential to lend was fully exhausted before. This will most likely include curtailing loan provisions to both domestic and foreign non-bank borrowers. At this point of the crisis, financial strains will impinge on the real economy. It is to be expected that interest rates would jump up drastically, thereby adding to recessionary pressures. The widespread cutback in lending will probably produce major economic shock waves resulting in severe reductions in production, employment and international trade on a worldwide scale.

What about the likelihood of a general run on banks and a collapse of the whole financial system? Johnson (1983, p. 12) argued:

in the absence of complete information about the affairs of banks in which they deposit their funds, depositors are naturally prone to become doubtful of banks in general when even a few banks are thought to be in serious trouble. Contagion is likely to be a more serious problem with respect to international than domestic deposits, because of the difficulties that some depositors have in obtaining information, the large size of individual deposits (which implies minimal coverage by any available deposit insurance), and uncertainty about the ability and willingness of national authorities to protect foreign depositors against loss in the event of a bank failure.

It has to be recalled, however, that monetary authorities in the creditor countries have instruments at their disposal to prevent a liquidity crisis and probable chain reactions. Central banks can announce in advance that they would counteract an increase in liquidity preferences of the public by maintaining the expansion of broad money supply. This would assure depositors that monetary authorities would not repeat the serious mistakes of the late twenties and early thirties. Under these circumstances it could be reasoned that a *general* run on banks is rather unlikely to occur. If it were guaranteed that the collapse of a few insolvent banks will not result in an overall shortage in liquidity, there would no longer be any reason for a general panic.

Preventing the worst does not mean that developing countries' defaults will not produce any international drawbacks at all. First, there is some controversy whether failures of some insolvent banks would have contractive effects on the economy, even if they are not permitted to reduce the money supply (Vaubel, 1984). Friedman, Schwartz (1967) and others concluded from historical analyses that it was the decline in the rate of monetary growth rather than bank failures by themselves which led to severe business contractions. On the other hand, authors like Bernanke (1983), Diamond and Dybvig (1983) and Kindleberger (1978) postulate that bank failures also depress the economy by raising the cost of credit intermediation. Bank failures are perceived as reducing aggregate demand and as interrupting production when loans are called. Against the latter suggestion it may be argued that increasing costs of credit intermediation are a mere reflection of the depositors' uncertainty about monetary policy reactions to bank failures. Accordingly, these problems can probably also be solved by a pre-announced commitment by central banks to maintain monetary expansion.

Another point deserves mentioning. It has been hypothesised that debt problems of developing countries may even produce major international drawbacks without triggering off any bank collapses at all. The argument takes the sudden shift in banks' policies towards the Third World in mid-1982 as a starting point (see Ch. 7). The reluctance of creditors to provide fresh money may force borrowers to constrain imports drastically. This would be in sharp contrast to the last decade, when most developing countries continued to expand their imports (see Ch. 6). Trade figures for 1982 and

1983 already pointed to a remarkable change in this respect. In nominal terms, imports of all NOPECs declined by $48 and $75 billion compared to 1981 values (i.e. by 11 and 17 per cent, respectively). According to some observers' concerns, this tendency, if it holds or even deteriorates, may endanger the international trading system as a whole (see Clausen, 1984). This, as a corollary, may severely depress the world economy.

In the remaining part of this chapter this reasoning will be discussed. As a first step, the hypothesis will be examined that banks indiscriminately refused to lend more money to developing countries, irrespective of the borrowers' different ability and willingness to service foreign debt. Second, the Third World's importance as an export market for the developed countries will be evaluated in order to gain an impression on possible international drawbacks of restrictive import policies in borrowing countries.

An insufficient extent of lending to borrowing countries has sometimes been made responsible for the severity of the Depression half a century ago (Arndt, 1944; Kindleberger, 1973, 1978). Concern is raised that this mistake may be repeated in the eighties. It is feared that banks may *voluntarily* decide to drastically cut credit provisions, in contrast to a credit contraction *enforced* by loan losses affecting the banks' capital base. Especially smaller banks seem to aim at reducing their exposure to the Third World.[3]

Most importantly, changes in banks' perception of country risk may display 'bandwagon' effects (Williams *et al.*, 1982, p. 16). Waves of pessimism following waves of enthusiasm may not only affect lending to individual borrowers with evident difficulties in servicing their debt, but also lending to rather sound debtors. On a regional basis such a process seems to have emerged recently.[4] Difficulties encountered by Colombia in raising further loans, for example, must be largely attributed to the financial distress of neighbouring Latin American borrowers (Hastings, 1983). The process of an indiscriminate refusal to continue lending may be further extended to sound debtors in other regions.

Moreover, for two reasons sound debtors may even be

more severely hit by the banks' reluctance to lend than problem borrowers. First, if banks neglect differences in risks of different borrowers (e.g. because it is too costly to evaluate them), this will result in a tendency to a uniform interest rate which reflects the *average* risk of loans to developing countries. This may induce a process of adverse selection. Sound and low-risk borrowers who find the average interest rate inordinately high will be driven out from international capital markets (de Grauwe, Fratianni, 1983). Second, banks were recently increasingly pressed by international organisations like the IMF to provide further credits for major problem borrowers. Such an 'involuntary' lending is likely to narrow the scope for lending to sound debtors in so far as bank regulations and precaution set limits to the banks' overall engagement in the Third World. Both factors would contribute considerably to a misallocation of capital on an international scale.

Quarterly data on net lending presented in Table 38 clearly point out the drastic change in bank behaviour in mid-1982. In the third quarter of 1982 net lending was negative for eleven out of eighteen sample countries. The fact that four members of the intermediate and the non-problem group of borrowers—Egypt, Korea, Malaysia, Thailand—were included may be stated in favour of the hypothesis of an indiscriminate refusal of banks to maintain credit relations. Compared to the second quarter, the amount of credits raised (net of repayments) declined to between 12 and 15 per cent for both the intermediate and the non-problem group. With regards to aggregated data for all non-Latin American NOPECs—which were not fully comparable to other data presented in Table 38 because only the aggregated figures are adjusted for exchange-rate effects—the shift was even more pronounced.

However, for the group of countries experiencing no major difficulties in servicing their foreign debt, the decline proved to be of a very short-term nature. Possibly, the borrowers themselves temporarily refrained from raising further capital in view of unfavourable credit conditions, rather than reluctant creditors resisting to provide new credits for them. Net lending significantly recovered in the

Table 38: Net Bank Lending to Major Third World Borrowing Countries, First Quarter 1981 to Third Quarter 1983 (in billions of US$)

	I/1981	II/1981	III/1981	IV/1981	I/1982	II/1982	III/1982	IV/1982	I/1983	II/1983	III/1983
Argentina	1.42	0.93	0.36	1.30	0.54	-0.57	-0.43	-0.32	0.51	0.28	0.02
Brazil	0.44	0.36	1.46	4.03	0.61	2.16	2.77	0.94	1.01	-0.01	0.08
Chile	0.47	0.72	1.00	0.72	0.28	0.77	-0.23	0.05	-0.45	-0.15	0.90
Colombia	-0.16	0.15	0.13	0.49	-0.43	0.50	0.17	0.44	-0.03	0.35	-0.05
Egypt	0.06	0.40	0.05	0.27	0.15	0.67	-0.44	0.05	-0.20	0.58	-0.26
India	0.10	-0.02	0.06	0.04	0.16	0.08	0.10	0.21	-0.08	0.21	-0.01
Indonesia	-0.15	-0.20	0.35	0.26	0.19	0.17	0.17	1.10	0.59	-0.21	0.38
Ivory Coast	-0.07	-0.06	0.12	0.08	-0.25	0.12	0.03	0.25	-0.25	0.10	0.13
Republic of Korea	0.53	1.05	0.04	1.26	-0.69	0.40	-0.19	2.43	-0.41	0.21	0.17
Malaysia	-0.05	0.08	0.32	0.61	0.14	0.40	-0.05	0.84	0.70	0.21	0.43
Mexico	1.73	2.21	4.96	5.60	2.70	3.68	-1.75	-1.17	1.12	0.36	1.08
Nigeria	0.12	0.20	0.97	0.06	0.00	0.71	0.60	0.96	0.70	0.16	0.05
Philippines	-0.37	-0.06	0.35	0.35	0.28	0.52	0.28	0.01	-0.06	0.63	-0.49
Thailand	0.04	-0.13	-0.15	0.32	-0.39	-0.05	-0.23	0.39	-0.05	0.28	0.14
Turkey	-0.10	-0.15	0.10	-0.04	-0.07	-0.12	-0.00	0.03	-0.03	-0.04	-0.01
Venezuela	0.20	-0.54	0.34	0.98	-0.02	0.26	-0.04	0.17	-0.43	-0.24	-0.51
Yugoslavia	0.16	-0.20	0.06	0.26	-0.54	-0.13	-0.36	0.45	-0.26	0.00	-0.28
Zaire	0.03	0.03	-0.03	0.01	-0.08	-0.05	-0.06	-0.07	0.01	-0.09	0.02
Problem borrowers[a]	4.35	3.36	8.25	12.86	3.42	6.00	-0.10	0.08	1.48	0.11	1.30
Intermediate group of borrowers[b]	0.27	1.53	1.53	2.02	-0.51	2.42	0.28	3.70	-0.22	1.68	-0.40
Non-problem borrowers[c]	-0.22	-0.12	0.71	1.72	-0.33	1.10	0.16	2.98	1.13	0.84	0.89
Memorandum items:											
Latin America[d]	4.5	4.9	8.7	12.4	4.1	7.7	1.3	-0.9	2.7	1.4	1.7
Other NOPECs[d]	0.1	2.8	2.1	4.4	-1.7	5.3	-2.0	6.0	-0.6	3.2	0.0

[a] Argentina, Brazil, Chile, Mexico, Turkey, Venezuela, Yugoslavia, Zaire.   [b] Egypt, Ivory Coast, Korea, Nigeria, Philippines.
[c] Colombia, India, Indonesia, Malaysia, Thailand.   [d] Adjusted for exchange-rate effects.

Source: BIS, *International Banking Developments.*

next quarter. Comparing averages for I.1981 to II.1982 on the one hand and III.1982 to III.1983 on the other hand, the quarterly amount of new credits raised by the five non-problem borrowers even increased from $0.5 billion to $1.2 billion. For the intermediate group of five borrowers, a small reduction of $0.2 billion to $1 billion was calculated. The development of net lending to the eight problem borrowers was in sharp contrast with this. Up to mid-1982, the latter group acquired an average quarterly amount of $6.4 billion in credits. Later on this figure dwindled to an average of $0.6 billion.

This leads us to conclude that at least up to September 1983 (more recent data were not available), the empirical evidence on net lending to developing countries reveals hardly any support for the hypothesis of an indiscriminate refusal of banks to provide further loans. A rather strong relationship emerges between the debt situation of borrowers and a continued access to international capital markets. In spite of 'involuntary' lending gaining momentum, problem borrowers run considerably short of fresh capital. Therefore, it is mainly this group of debtors which can be expected to constrain imports drastically in order to reduce balance of payments deficits.

Actually, the decline in imports remained rather modest for those ten sample countries not classified as problem borrowers (Table 39). On the other hand, the eight problem borrowers included in the sample accounted for nearly half of the import reduction of all NOPECs in 1982. Compared to import values of 1981, this group cut world market purchases down by 24 per cent (1982) and 30 per cent (1983). The relative reduction was roughly twice as high as for all NOPECs. The shift in import policies was most dramatic in some Latin American problem countries where recent import values sometimes amounted to only 60–45 per cent of figures of 1981 (for probable negative effects of drastic import reductions on economic growth and export expansion in the longer run and for a critique of the IMF's policy prescriptions in this respect, see pp. 70 and 150).

In order to evaluate possible consequences of the decline in developing countries' imports for the international trading

Table 39: Change in Imports for Major Third World Borrowing Countries, 1982 and 1983 vis-à-vis 1981

	1982		1983[a]	
	billions of US$	in percent of 1981 values	billions of US$	in percent of 1981 values
Argentina	−4.09	−43.4	−4.75	−50.3
Brazil	−3.01	−12.5	−6.66	−27.7
Chile	−2.84	−44.6	−3.64	−57.1
Mexico	−9.51	−39.5	n.a.	n.a.
Turkey	−0.07	−0.8	0.23	2.6
Venezuela	−0.53	−4.1	−2.83	−21.6
Yugoslavia	−2.38	−15.0	−3.73	−23.6
Zaire	−0.19	−28.1	n.a.	n.a.
All eight problem borrowers	−22.62	−23.5[b]	n.a.	−29.6[b]
Remaining ten sample countries	−5.44	−2.2[b]	n.a.	−14.2[b,c]

[a] With the exception of Venezuela, estimated on the basis of quarterly data of fourth quarter 1982 to third quarter 1983.
[b] Unweighted average.
[c] For seven borrowers only; Egypt, Indonesia and Malaysia had to be neglected because of data limitations.

Source: IMF, *International Financial Statistics*.

system, it has to be considered that the Third World's world-market share is still relatively small. In the early eighties nominal imports of all NOPECs accounted for a little bit more than one-fifth of world trade. The developing countries' role (OPEC countries included) as export markets differed remarkably between major industrial economies, however (Table 40). It was negligible for Canada, about 25 per cent of total exports for Germany and the United Kingdom, but not much less than 50 per cent for Japan and the United States.

Although our sample of eighteen countries accounted for only one third of developed countries' exports to the Third World, it can be concluded from figures presented in Table 40 that exports to problem borrowers were of rather minor importance to most developed economies. The share of eight major problem debtors included in the sample in total exports did not exceed 5 per cent, with the only exception of

Table 40: Developed Countries' Exports to Developing Countries, 1981 (in percent of total exports)[a]

	All developing countries	Eighteen sample countries[c]	Eight problem borrowers[c]	Memorandum item: Share of total exports in GDP (in percent)
Canada	12.7	5.2	3.2	23.3
France	33.4	6.9	3.0	17.7
Germany, Federal Republic of	24.6	7.7	4.1	25.7
Japan	49.7	17.5	3.6	13.3
United Kingdom[b]	26.9	7.0	2.1	21.7
United States	44.0	21.1	13.5	7.9

[a] Merchandise exports only.
[b] 1980.
[c] Excluded are borrowers with only marginal trade relations with reporting industrial countries.

Sources: UN, *Yearbook of International Trade Statistics*; IMF, *International Financial Statistics*.

the United States. The relatively high share of 13.5 per cent for the latter country is a reflection of its strong trade relations with Latin America. Accordingly, the direct impact of drastic import reductions by problem borrowers will be largely concentrated on the United States and will be felt considerably less elsewhere. Even for the United States, however, only 1.1 per cent of GDP directly hinges on merchandise exports to the eight problem borrowers (0.011 = 0.135 · 0.079; for a similar calculation, see Weintraub, 1983a, p. 33). Accounting for indirect effects, the impact will still remain rather weak. If the usual multiplier effects in industrial countries are applied, the impact on GDP will roughly double (Franko, 1979, p. 292).

Notwithstanding that import reductions by developing countries adversely affect international trade and add to economic difficulties in industrialised economies, it is unlikely that they will strongly depress economic activity on an international scale. The major problem borrowers' role in international trade seems to be too small to trigger a severe contraction in world exports, even if creditor banks continue to resist further loan demands and borrowers are forced to constrain imports for several years.

This conclusion is subject to a crucial qualification, however. It only holds if restrictive import policies of borrowers experiencing acute balance of payments troubles will not induce widespread contagion effects. If industrial countries faced by export losses aim at taking revenge (instead of adjusting their own economies) this may, before long, result in an upward spiral of international protectionism, which, as a corollary, may lead to a downward spiral of international trade and economic activity. As in the case of the possible consequences of bank failures, the extent of international drawbacks arising from debt problems of developing countries again heavily depends on policy reactions in *creditor* countries. If both central banks and governments in the industrialised world avoid severe policy failures (i.e., most importantly, if they maintain monetary expansion and resist protectionist pressures), worldwide drawbacks will be largely limited. On the other hand, if they repeat former mistakes, another world economic crisis becomes probable.

NOTES

1.   For an estimate of the capital of banks in the BIS reporting area, *see* Johnson, 1983, p. 10; the figure given there is $335 billion at the end of 1981.
2.   For a further elaboration of this argument, *see* Sjaastad, 1983, pp. ·316–18.
3.   For a theoretical backing of this argument, *see* de Grauwe, Fratianni, 1983; Sachs, Cohen, 1982.
4.   This is why the conclusion of Franko may be questioned; that is, an indiscriminate refusal of banks to lend is 'found unlikely in a world in which the differences in borrowers real abilities to service debt through foreign exchange earnings are recognized' (1979, p. 294).

Part IV
POSSIBLE SOLUTIONS

10 Debt Rescheduling and the Role of the IMF

It is still open to question whether policy-makers in the industrialised world are well prepared against repeating mistakes that fifty years ago caused economic difficulties to result in a severe worldwide depression. Similarly it seems rather dubious whether the borrowing countries in the Third World and the Western lending banks have already learnt their lessons from the difficulties in handling international debt in the recent past. All parties involved were nearly exclusively concerned with short-term emergency measures. Policy reactions capable of tackling the underlying causes of the Third World's debt problems clearly receded into the background.

Frequently it is argued that emergency programmes serve to gain time in order to devise lasting solutions in the meantime. In this chapter the short-term actions of the recent past will be critically reviewed. Special emphasis is given to the role the IMF is playing in the process of rescheduling. Subsequently, in Chapter 11, the question will be posed whether it makes sense to postpone debt-service obligations via rescheduling. The success of this strategy critically hinges on a significant improvement in international economic conditions in the near future. Finally, some important and interesting proposals will be discussed which may contribute to a longer-term solution of debt problems and which thereby may fill the aforementioned policy gap (Chs. 12 and 13).

The sharp increase in developing countries' external payments arrears that occurred in the early eighties and the growing demands for rescheduling have already been stated elsewhere (see p. 122).[1] The way these requests were dealt with differed according to the creditors who were addressed. Debt owed to *official* creditors was normally renegotiated

141

under the aegis of the Paris Club, the most important club of official creditors. For this purpose no formal organisation based on internationally agreed criteria has been established. The institutional framework has remained an informal one and the restructuring approach has been on a pragmatic, case-by-case basis (Nowzad, Williams *et al.*, 1981, p. 22). Nevertheless, some regularities in official debt renegotiations have evolved over the years (Brau, Williams *et al.*, 1983, p. 10):

1. Generally, both principal and interest payments on medium-term and long-term loans falling due during a given period, including those already in arrears, were rescheduled, though not on terms that might be regarded as concessionary.
2. The Paris Club generally refused to reschedule payments on short-term debt.
3. The period of consolidation (i.e. the period in which payments to be restructured fall due) was normally twelve months. Sometimes, however, debt relief was also granted on successive occasions.
4. As regards the terms for repayment, the major portion of rescheduled debt, usually between 80 and 90 per cent of the total, normally carried a maturity of seven to nine years, with a grace period of three to four years.
5. The terms of repayment for rescheduled arrears were normally more stringent and the portion rescheduled was less than that for payments falling due.
6. The details of debt relief were bilaterally arranged between the debtor and each creditor country on the basis of guidelines which ensured that the terms were broadly uniform for different creditors.
7. The debtor country was asked to take measures to restore its financial viability. For this purpose, arrangements with the IMF had to be concluded.

As regards the restructuring of (officially non-guaranteed) debt owed to *private* creditors, the number of countries that have approached the Western commercial banks for relief has in recent times increased sharply. By October 1983 five of the ten largest Third World borrowers had either completed or were engaged in multilateral negotiations on debt rescheduling with commercial banks. The total amount of restructured bank-debt reached $60 billion in 1983 through early October (Brau, Williams *et al.*, 1983, pp. 1, 11). Brau, Williams *et al.* identified the following typical features of commercial bank debt-restructurings (1983, p. 12):

1. In contrast to official reschedulings, the restructuring of bank debt has been restricted to principal payments falling due or already in arrears. Only in exceptional cases interest payments in arrears were also rescheduled.

2. On the other hand, banks were willing to include short-term debt in rescheduling arrangements, which the Paris Club generally refused.

3. As in Paris Club agreements, the period of consolidation was normally twelve months—with only some exceptions, where consolidation was extended up to two to three years.

4. Largely comparable to official reschedulings, generally at least 80 per cent of total principal payments falling due were restructured, carrying maturities of seven to eight years in most instances, though with a somewhat shorter grace period of two to three years.

5. On occasion, the terms of repayment for both short-term loans included and rescheduled arrears were more stringent in so far as maturities were shorter.

6. Commercial banks refused to reschedule debt at less than market-related interest rates. In the period 1978–83, the spread over LIBOR charged on consolidated debt ranged from 1.75 to 2.25 per cent. In addition, restructuring fees of between 1 and 1.5 per cent of the amounts restructured were charged.

7. Frequently banks agreed to provide additional financing, or at least gave assurances that they would not reduce their exposure. The conditions for new lending were quite similar to rescheduling terms.

8. Additionally, bridging finance was granted in some cases by commercial banks, by governments of industrialised countries or by the Bank for International Settlements acting on behalf of major Western central banks.

9. Similar to official Paris Club creditors, commercial banks generally made rescheduling agreements conditional upon negotiations of the borrower with the IMF on upper credit tranche arrangements.

The quick response of both official and private creditors to the mounting difficulties in debt servicing of developing countries in the early eighties is widely regarded as having been successful (see Cline, 1983, pp. 40–44; Deutsche Bundesbank, 1984, p. 81). The mood of panic which culminated after the Mexican payment crisis in August 1982 has now cooled. It surely has to be admitted that the emergency programmes have so far prevented the international financial system from being significantly affected by the Third World's debt problems. Debt restructuring helped the commercial banks to confine write-offs of poor loans to an extent which remained easily manageable. Moreover, under the restructuring arrangements some borrowing countries committed themselves to embark on substantial adjustment measures. In some instances, progress has already been achieved (see, additionally, Clausen, 1983, p. 258).

Yet there is reason enough to question the economic soundness of the rescheduling approach, which implicitly assumes that the debt problems of major borrowers are of a liquidity nature rather than of a solvency nature.[2] Evidently, restructuring cannot solve debt problems but only gains time. The recent postponement of repayments is expected to result in 'a "hump" in debt-service obligations between 1985 and 1987' (Clausen, 1984, p. 10). Apart from scepticism about the likelihood of an improvement in economic conditions for transferring debt-service payments in future (Ch. 11), and apart from doubts whether the time gained has actually been used to design appropriate longer-term solutions (Ch. 12), several aspects of recent reschedulings are open to a more inherent criticism.[3]

First, a rather long time-lag between the identification of debt difficulties and a negotiated settlement has been observed in some cases (Nowzad, Williams *et al.*, 1981, pp. 34, 38). Hardy concluded from a review of past debt reschedulings that the response of creditors to borrowers' requests for debt relief 'was delayed until arrears had accumulated and the prospect of outright default or suspension of all debt-service payments was imminent' (Hardy, 1982, p. 33). On average, discussions between the borrowing countries and the creditor banks began as late as one to two years after the time a debt problem might have been identified (because of arrears in debt servicing or because of the banks' reluctance to continue lending). Another one to three years elapsed before a restructuring agreement was finally signed.

It has to be considered, however, that the two reviews just referred to do not include reschedulings of the most recent past. Time lags in the creditors' reactions seem to have shortened considerably, at least in the most important cases which threatened the banks' financial position. Organisational difficulties of debt restructuring were rather efficiently dealt with. The task of coordination between the huge number of creditor banks (that in some instances amounted to several hundreds) was performed by steering committees of bankers. Previous experiences have led to some further standardisation in the framework and approach adopted. In those instances where time-lags still remained unduly long (e.g. because final agreement was delayed by creditors unable to reach a consensus on continued lending or by borrowers struggling with the IMF for less harsh adjustment programmes) bridging finance frequently eased financial tensions in the short run.

Therefore, a second point seems more important. As noted earlier, most of recent reschedulings were restricted to one year's amortisation payments. It may be argued that in this way the borrowing countries were held in short leash, thereby enforcing compliance to economic policy commitments earlier agreed upon (Cline, 1983, p.86). However, since most debtors continue to depend on the provision of fresh bank loans, which may be refused in case of borrowers not meeting their commitments, lenders' leverage can be maintained even without insisting on extremely short consolidation periods in rescheduling arrangements. On the other hand, the prolongation of consolidation periods may bring advantage by providing a reasonable planning horizon for borrowers and by taking into account their medium-term economic prospects (Feldstein, 1984, p. 10).

The recurrence of debt-servicing problems, sometimes only shortly after a rescheduling had been arranged (see Table 19, pp. 46–7) clearly points to the short-sightedness of the approach applied in the past. One of the most impressive recent examples in this respect was Argentina. In early 1983 a financial rescue package for Argentina was signed, comprising of $7 billion principal payments rescheduled (in arrears at the end of 1982 and due in 1983) plus $1.5 billion new medium-term bank loans, a bridging loan and an IMF standby arrangement (see Brau, Williams *et al.*, 1983, pp. 35–42). And just over twelve months later Argentina was again considerably lagging behind in debt servicing, overdue interest payments totalling $2.7 billion (*The Financial Times*, 30 March 1984). Only another emergency programme prevented the declaration of loans as non-performing which might have significantly hurt US banks' profits at least in the first quarter of 1984.[4]

Against this background it may be concluded that the extremely short-term rescheduling approach which dominated in the recent past resulted in a mere muddling-through. Human resources were nearly permanently absorbed in new and renewed emergency actions. It seems that reschedulings largely failed in gaining sufficient time to devise longer-term solutions of debt problems in the meanwhile.

Third, it remains to be discussed whether the rescheduling approach, as applied in the past, has provided economically sound incentives as regards the burden sharing, both within the group of creditors and among creditors, borrowers, taxpayers and consumers. Turning to the question of burden sharing within the banking system first, the free rider problem or incoherence problem has to be addressed: 'An individual creditor does not want to concede grace periods or commit additional funds unless the debtor would promise not to use the resulting leeway to repay other creditors' (Vaubel, 1983, p. 299). Smaller banks, in particular, recently tried to reduce their exposure to highly indebted developing countries by refusing to participate in restructuring arrangements and to provide fresh loans proportionate to their existing respective exposures. This behaviour seems merely rational from the individual bank's point of view. Its individual action is rather irrelevant as regards the probability of the borrower's default; that is, the *micro-economic* condition for continued lending is not met. Only the individual decisions of a few large and highly engaged banks significantly influence the probability of default (Cline, 1983, pp. 78–81). In other words, a strong incentive exists for smaller banks to withdraw from lending at the expense of some large banks. The risk of claims held by the remaining large banks increases, which induces more creditors to discontinue lending.

The banks' recent tendency to shorten the maturity of their loans and their insistence on extremely short consolidation periods in reschedulings may be interpreted as an attempt to escape this dilemma (de Grauwe, Fratianni, 1983, pp. 19–21). However, what seems to be rational from a micro-economic point of view, namely improving the possibility of quickly withdrawing from credit engagements regarded as critical, cannot solve the problem. All banks reacting in the same way means that no individual bank gains a better position than all other creditors. Moreover, the sum of individual precautionary measures may even aggravate the problem for the whole system. The banks' reactions may result in a severe bunching of maturities for the borrowing country which increases the probability of its default.

Several ways can be thought about how to deal with free riding more effectively. Individual creditors may make offers to maintain or even expand their exposure conditional on the conclusion of similar agreements with other creditors (Vaubel, 1983b, p. 299). If this approach is rejected because of high transaction costs arising from the huge number of creditors involved, large banks may force smaller banks to join reschedulings by announcing that non-participating creditors will be excluded from syndications at better times in the future. The borrowing countries, too, may exert some pressure on banks reluctant to continue lending (Cline, 1983, p. 80). Retaliatory measures may again take the form of permanently cutting off credit relations with non-participating banks. Moreover, the borrower may even threaten reluctant lenders to treat their loans less favourably than those of banks willing to cooperate.

But these approaches still have some shortcomings. The subordination of loans just mentioned is difficult to enforce because syndicated loan agreements typically include cross-default clauses. Furthermore, the capital market's confidence in the borrower may be largely eroded by such an announcement. The exclusion of non-participating banks from future lending requires lasting coherence among different participating banks as well as among the group of participating banks and the borrowing country. The theory and history of cartels tells us that this is a rather unrealistic assumption. If the exclusion strategy succeeds, this may result in a misallocation of capital since cartel-outsiders are driven out from certain lending markets.

Possibly it is partly due to these difficulties that international organisations—especially the IMF—have been referred to in the past to ensure an effective collective bank response to the developing countries' demands for rescheduling.[5] In fact, the IMF has been successful on several occasions in pressing reluctant banks to maintain or even increase their exposure. The IMF's role in this context was however not restricted to that of a coordinating agent assisting the formation of bank consortia or 'clubs'. In addition, the IMF interfered in the second aspect of burden sharing; that is, the process of burden sharing among lenders, borrowers and the public. This happened in two ways: first, by prescribing economic policy adjustments to countries asking for debt restructuring and, second, by granting official funds as part of rescue packages.

Has the IMF gone too far? It may be argued that the more compulsory the IMF pressures on banks to maintain lending have become in the past, the more banks may claim official bail-outs if repayment difficulties of developing countries continue and banks can no longer circumvent the realisation of losses (Cline, 1983, p. 80). It seems plausible that banks have been eager to gain IMF assistance in organising collective action since this approach has simultaneously offered the opportunity of socialising losses later on. A portion of the burden may have been shifted to the public already: debt restructuring operations 'so far have been widely and not too unfairly caricatured as a process designed to rescue banks rather than debtors' (*The Financial Times*, 2 May 1984). What has been concluded by Hardy (1982, pp. 25–30) for official reschedulings under the aegis of the Paris Club—namely, that the creditors' financial costs of debt relief were not very high—seems all the more true for private creditors:[6] 'Estimates indicate that private creditors have probably not suffered a financial loss [through re-schedulings] on a present value basis' (Group of Thirty, 1982, p. 14). If there was any burden of reschedulings for the banks to bear, Holthus (1984, p. 50) finds reason to believe that this has at least partly been socialised, for example by restraining domestic competition which allowed artificially high charges to be levied on domestic bank customers.

This is not to blame commercial banks for insisting on market terms in reschedulings; otherwise developing countries would have faced even more difficulties in obtaining the banks' cooperation and incentives for 'involuntary' lending would have been significantly reduced. However, where commercial banks have formerly not assured themselves that the borrowers would be able to service their foreign debt, they have to bear the consequences (Williamson, 1982, p. 56). Lenders should not be officially bailed out, neither by the IMF nor in other ways (see also Ch. 12) because this would result in a severe moral hazard problem. If losses arising from international lending are taken over by the public, commercial banks can disregard risks and stick to macro-economically imprudent lending practices.

As regards the IMF's engagement in reschedulings, a clear distinction has to be drawn between the formulation of economic policy conditions and its own financial role, notwithstanding that both elements have an impact on the burden sharing among the different parties involved. Economic policies typically prescribed by the IMF (for the design of adjustment programmes, see Williamson, 1982, pp. 25–36) frequently imply considerable adjustment burdens for the borrowing countries. It can hardly be doubted, however, that domestic policy failures which have formerly contributed to the emergence of debt problems should be corrected without further delay.

Generally, borrowers should have sufficient incentives to adopt the necessary policies on their own. A painful re-orientation in economic policies is however frequently resisted by important pressure groups within the country. This is why the IMF's role sometimes goes beyond merely advising economic policy changes. The IMF's involve-ment—making the availability of further bank lending con-ditional on adjustment measures—may help the internal enforcement by serving as an 'ideal bogeyman to be blamed for unpopular policy changes' (Vaubel, 1983b, p. 299).

Broadly speaking, the design of IMF adjustment pro-grammes seems well suited to improve domestic policies of borrowing countries. Requirements to constrain govern-ments' budget deficits, to suppress inflation, to correct overvalued and heavily fluctuating exchange rates and to encourage export production, for example, are largely in line with the reasoning presented in Chapter 6. In some respects, however, the rules of adjustment imposed by the IMF seem ill-conceived. Especially demands to reduce imports may shift the debt problem from one country to another. Frequently one problem borrower's imports are another problem borrower's exports, as in the case of Argentina, Brazil and Mexico where trade linkages are extensive (Meltzer, 1983, pp. 3–4). At least in some in-stances, the IMF policies seemed to be rather strongly concentrated on *short-run* improvements in the balance of payments position, which may have led to unduly high losses in income and employment (Williamson, 1982, p. 53). An extension of the standard one-year programmes to longer-term programmes may help to reduce these losses by permitting a better balance of payments performance at broadly sustained income levels (see, additionally, Khan, Knight, 1981, pp. 41–4; Crockett, 1981, pp. 70–3).

Parallel to the formulation of adjustment programmes, the IMF has considerably increased its lending (Table 41). Net of borrowers' repayments, IMF lending doubled from $5.5 billion in 1981 to $11.3 billion two years later. The expansion was not restricted to credits which were available

Table 41: Lending by the International Monetary Fund, 1980–83[a] (in billions of US$)

	1980	1981	1982	1983
Gross lending	4.4	8.0	8.2	13.5
Credit tranche drawings	2.3	4.0	2.8	5.2
Extended facility drawings	0.8	2.5	2.3	4.9
Compensatory financing	1.3	1.4	2.9	3.0
Buffer stock facility	—	—	0.1	0.3
Repayments	4.3	2.5	2.0	2.1
Net lending	0.3	5.5	6.4	11.3

[a] Minor discrepancies due to rounding.

Source: Deutsche Bundesbank, 1984.

only if the borrowers adhered to economic policy conditions, but also took place in (low-conditionality) compensatory financing (for the distinction of unconditional, low-conditionality and high-conditionality financing, see Table 42 and Williamson, 1982, pp. 64–7). As regards total liquidity creation by the IMF, nominal figures nearly quadrupled in the period 1975–83 (Table 42). Even in real terms, liquidity creation doubled after 1975, notwithstanding that with the collapse of the Bretton Woods system of fixed exchange rates in 1973 it could be expected that the need for IMF lending would be considerably diminished (Vaubel, 1983b, p. 291).

Quite recently it was decided to further increase international liquidity. Credit commitments of the Group of Ten countries under the General Arrangement to Borrow (which in future are also available for conditional financing by the IMF) were raised from SDR 6.4 billion to SDR 17 billion. Only shortly afterwards (February 1983) it was agreed to increase total IMF-member quotas by almost 50 per cent to SDR 90 billion.

In contrast to the conventional wisdom which welcomes the IMF's enlarged financial engagement (see Clausen, 1984, p. 11; Cline, 1983, pp. 105–8; Deutsche Bundesbank, 1984, pp. 88–90; Crockett, 1981, p. 65), some important objections may be raised against an increased IMF lending. Even if the argument holds that there is a temporary need for more international liquidity, this would not justify a

Table 42: International Liquidity Creation by the International Monetary Fund, 1970–83 (outstanding at end of period)

	1970	1975	1980	1981	1982	1983
Unconditional liquidity						
Net cumulative allocations of SDRs						
in billions of SDRs	3.4	9.3	17.4	21.4	21.4	21.4
in billions of 1970 US$	3.4	7.9	11.4	11.6	10.4	9.5
as percent of total	51.5	52.3	52.3	44.3	41.6	32.2
Low-conditionality liquidity[a]						
Compensatory financing (in billions of SDRs)	0.1	0.7	2.8	3.3	5.4	7.5
Buffer stock facility (in billions of SDRs)	—	0.0	—	—	0.1	0.4
Oil facility (in billions of SDRs)	—	4.8	1.9	0.9	0.1	—
Trust fund loans (in billions of SDRs)	—	—	1.3	0.4	3.0	2.9
Subtotal						
in billions of SDRs	0.1	5.5	6.0	4.6	8.6	10.8
in billions of 1970 US$	0.1	4.7	3.9	2.5	4.2	4.8
as percent of total	1.5	31.1	17.9	9.5	16.8	16.3
High-conditionality liquidity[b]						
Credit tranche drawings (in billions of SDRs)	2.9	1.8	2.6	6.0	8.4	12.2
Extended facility drawings (in billions of SDRs)	—	0.0	1.1	3.1	5.3	9.8
Undrawn balances under:						
Stand-by arrangements (in billions of SDRs)	0.2	1.0	2.3	3.8	3.1	4.5
Extended arrangements (in billions of SDRs)	—	0.1	3.9	9.3	4.6	7.9
Subtotal						
in billions of SDRs	3.1	2.9	9.9	22.2	21.4	34.4
in billions of 1970 US$	3.1	2.5	6.5	12.1	10.4	15.2
as percent of total	47.0	16.6	29.8	46.2	41.6	51.5
Total liquidity creation						
in billions of SDRs	6.6	17.7	33.3	48.2	51.4	66.6
in billions of 1970 US$	6.6	15.1	21.7	26.2	25.0	29.5
as percent of world exports	2.3	2.6	2.3	3.0	3.3	4.2

[a] First credit tranche excluded.
[b] First credit tranche included.

Sources: IMF, 1982; IMF, *International Financial Statistics*.

permanent (additional) liquidity expansion (Brunner *et al.*, 1983, p.166). Furthermore, concessional IMF lending is likely to create another moral hazard problem, this time on the borrowers' side (Vaubel, 1983b; Sjaastad, 1983, pp. 318–20).[7] If rescheduling is granted at concessional terms, because the IMF steps in and extends subsidised loans, this will probably invite further demands for re-scheduling and encourage more countries to threaten with default. There is a danger that mismanagement of borrowers will be rewarded and economic policy adjustment will be further postponed. Moreover, the relatively favourable terms of IMF lending provide an incentive for borrowers to treat the IMF as a lender of first rather than of last resort (Williamson, 1982, pp. 17–18).

Against borrowing in international capital markets, the provision of funds by the IMF has the further disadvantage of expanding the worldwide money supply. Figures in Table 42 show that liquidity creation by the IMF has sharply increased, both in real terms and as a share of world exports. Therefore it is likely that IMF lending gives rise to additional inflationary pressures. In other words, through IMF lending, part of the burden arising from developing countries' debt problems is shifted to consumers whose real incomes are reduced.

To sum up, then, tendencies to shift the burden of adjustment from lenders and borrowers to groups that are hardly able to counter such attempts (because their interests are difficult to organise) should be resisted. The IMF's role in rescheduling developing countries' debts should be defined in a way that does not encourage moral hazard either on the lenders' or the borrowers' side. Above all, this requires a revision of IMF lending practices. Otherwise it is to be expected that possible short-term alleviations of debt problems will be counter-productive in the longer run; by triggering new and renewed cases of default and demands for official bail-outs, debt problems are likely to further deteriorate.

NOTES

1. For further details, *see* Brau, Williams *et al.*, 1983; Nowzad, Williams *et al.*, 1981; Mendelsohn, 1983.

2. The distinction between illiquidity and insolvency has been elaborated in Aliber, 1980; *see*, additionally, Sjaastad, 1983, pp. 316–18.

3. For a harsh critique of the conventional approach of debt restructuring and alternative suggestions, *see* Abbott, 1979, pp. 189–246.

4. The programme included $300 million in loans granted by four other Latin American nations—Brazil, Colombia, Mexico and Venezuela. The US government agreed to lend $300 million once Argentina signed a new arrangement with the IMF. This loan was scheduled to repay the aforementioned loans. In addition, US commercial banks provided $100 million at unusually low interest rates (*The Wall Street Journal*, 2 April 1984).

5. The need for some form of collective action is also stressed in Sachs, 1983. Joint bank action can also be enforced by Western central banks. This would require a second step of coordination, however; namely, among different national agencies which, in a first step, have organised collective bank action on a national level.

6. The total amount of costs to the creditors arising from debt relief granted to developing countries in the period 1956–81 is estimated as $2 billion. Since 1975 there has been no loss at all.

7. Although the share of high-conditionality liquidity has remarkably increased recently (Table 42) and the subsidisation of SDR use has been reduced (by raising its interest rate towards market levels), still a considerable degree of subsidisation is inherent in IMF lending to developing countries. Concessional assistance can be obtained from the Oil Facility Subsidy Account, the Supplementary Financing Facility Subsidy Account and the Trust Fund. Loans in the credit tranches and under the compensatory financing and buffer-stock financing facilities are also available at periodic rates of charge that are concessionary when compared with market rates of interest (Gold, 1979; IMF, *Annual Report*, 1982, p. 117, Table I.11). Even IMF lending at average market rates of interest includes a subsidy for those borrowers that represent a relatively high risk, since the IMF does not levy different charges for different risks.

11   Hope for Improvement in International Economic Conditions

It makes sense to postpone debt-servicing payments via rescheduling and similar emergency measures only if there are reasonable prospects that economic conditions with respect to transferring interest and amortisation payments will significantly improve in future. Whether debt-service obligations will become easier to handle in the course of the eighties depends on the degree and success of internal adjustment within borrowing countries on the one hand and on the development of a favourable external economic environment on the other.

Although internal adjustment is frequently enforced by IMF conditionality, it is highly questionable that a re-orientation of domestic policies by borrowers will substantially ease their debt problems in the short run. Not all important debtor countries have asked for IMF credit tranches, the access to which is subject to an agreement on economic policies to be implemented by the borrower. Others who have themselves principally submitted to IMF programmes do not fully comply with the rules imposed and do not or cannot conduct themselves in accordance with the prescriptions originally agreed upon. Furthermore, the appropriateness of certain elements of IMF conditionality for alleviating debt difficulties is strongly disputed by some observers (see Ch. 10). Finally, and perhaps most importantly, even policy changes widely regarded as urgently required are unlikely to become effective in the short run. Since former policy failures have probably led to far-reaching distortions, it is rather to be expected that a re-orientation will need several years to substantially alleviate the debt situation of highly indebted Third World economies.

This is why hopes for a short-term solution to borrowing countries' financial strains can probably only be realised if the international economic environment for servicing foreign debt significantly improves without further delay. The following four factors seems to be most critical in this respect:

1. A recovery in economic growth in industrial countries.
2. A firm resistance to further protectionist pressures especially in the industrialised world and a commitment to gradually liberalise restrictive import practices which were formerly imposed.
3. A reduction in international interest rates.
4. A decline in prices for imported oil.

Both a better growth performance of industrial countries and a removal of barriers to external trade are supposed to enhance borrowing countries' exports. This would reduce deficits in the balance of current accounts and the borrowers' demands for capital imports in world financial markets. In addition, increased world-market sales may help to restore the developing countries' credit-worthiness, since this contributes to an improvement in debt and debt-service indicators. Declining international interest rates would alleviate the debt-service burden for new credits, for debt rescheduled at terms adjusted for changed capital-market conditions and for loans formerly raised at flexible interest rates. Lower petroleum prices would be favourable for net oil importing borrowers. Where petroleum imports form a major part of total imports, the reduction in current-account deficits may be remarkable.

In what follows, some rather crude estimates will be presented with respect to possible balance of payments effects of assumed improvements in external conditions. Furthermore, the likelihood of favourable developments with regard to the different factors mentioned above will be discussed. Finally, some projections and simulations—portraying future developments in the Third World's foreign indebtedness—will be briefly compared and critically reviewed.

Turning first to the impact a recovery in economic growth in industrial countries may have on NOPECs' export sales, two equations have been estimated. A trend equation run for different periods clearly shows the two-fold reduction in real growth rates of OECD countries after the first oil-price crisis and in the late seventies (Table 43).[1] A simple import

Table 43: Regression Coefficients: Annual Average OECD Growth Rates and Income Elasticities of OECD Imports from Non-Oil Developing Countries[a]

	Period of estimation:		
	1960–73	1974–78	1978–82
OECD growth rates	0.047	0.033	0.014
OECD import elasticities	1.818[b]	1.755	2.264[c]

[a] All coefficients significant at 5 per cent level of confidence or better; for the specification of equations estimated, see the text.
[b] 1967–73.
[c] 1974–82.

Sources: IMF, *International Financial Statistics*; UN, *Monthly Bulletin of Statistics*; own calculations.

function reveals the relationship between NOPEC exports to developed economies and OECD income.[2] The effects of different OECD growth paths on real NOPEC exports may now be calculated by applying the import elasticity prevailing in 1974–82 to different hypothetical OECD income levels. If extremely low economic growth rates of 1.4 per cent experienced in the most recent past persist in the coming years, NOPEC exports would only increase by 3.2 per cent ($0.0317 = 2.264 \cdot 0.014$). If the OECD succeeds, however, in returning to 1974–78 growth rates, or even to 1960–73 growth rates, the annual expansion in export volumes would rise to 7.5 or 10.6 per cent, respectively.

The prospective export developments under different growth scenarios are presented in Table 44. It is shown that a recovery of OECD growth to a level of 1960–73 would result in additional exports of $27.5 billion in 1984 (in prices of 1980). Two years later this effect would have more than doubled. The high growth scenario is rather unrealistic, however. It seems most unlikely that OECD

Table 44: Developments of Non-Oil Developing Countries' Exports under Different OECD Growth Scenarios,[a] 1984–86 (in billions of US$)

	Real exports			Difference in real exports	
	High (1)	Medium (2)	Low (3)	(1)–(3)	(2)–(3)
1984	204.1	192.1	176.6	27.5	15.5
1985	226.5	206.7	182.2	44.3	24.5
1986	251.3	222.5	188.0	63.3	34.5

[a] High: annual OECD growth rates of 4.7 per cent, as in 1960–73; medium: 3.3 per cent as in 1974–78; low: 1.4 per cent as in 1978–82.

Source: Own calculations.

economies will return to growth rates of the sixties and early seventies in the near future. According to projections presented by international organisations like the OECD, the IMF and the World Bank, annual growth rates in industrial countries in the second third of the eighties will probably be in the range of between 3 and 3.5 per cent. These forecasts conform quite well with scenario 2 in Table 44 which assumes a recovery of economic growth to rates prevailing in the period 1974–78. Although additional export sales are roughly halved under more realistic growth projections compared to the high-growth scenario, the balance of payments alleviation remains considerable. Additional exports of $15.5 (1984) to $34.5 billion (1986) would amount to between 18 and 39 per cent of average annual deficits in the NOPECs' balance of current accounts prevailing in the early eighties.

Besides the export-augmenting effect just mentioned, a favourable development of OECD growth may further reduce new borrowing needs of NOPECs and strengthen their capacity to service maturing loans. It may be argued that not only export volumes but also export prices of NOPECs would be positively affected. However, a quantification of the latter effect seems hardly possible. Moreover, it is only an improvement in terms-of-trade rather than an export-price rise which would help to ease balance of payments strains. Whether higher growth rates in OECD countries would lead to an increase in NOPECs' export prices high enough to outpace inflationary effects on the import side is even more difficult to assess. According to Cline (1983, pp. 47–8), NOPECs' terms-of-trade will not change once the OECD countries have reached a stable growth path. Only at times of rising growth rates will NOPEC exports tend to experience relatively large price increases. On the other hand, times of declining growth rates will see deteriorating terms-of-trade. Accordingly, possible terms-of-trade induced improvements in the balance of payments position are likely to be rather limited in time.

A recovery in OECD growth may furthermore result in a reduction of protectionist pressures. This again could add to export gains calculated above. Surprisingly, estimates of income elasticities of OECD imports from NOPECs (run for different sub-periods of the last fifteen years) do not indicate a remarkable decline in elasticities due to the mounting protectionism in the seventies (Table 43). Indeed elasticities were slightly reduced in 1974–78 compared to the period 1967–73, but increased considerably in the late seventies and early eighties. Most probably, elasticities would have further increased if industrial countries had resisted protectionist demands. On the other hand, the estimates may hint at time-lags in the effectiveness of trade restrictions. This means that possible liberalisations induced by an improved growth performance in industrial economies would likewise contribute to an easing of balance of payments problems for NOPECs with some delay only. Accordingly, considerable trade effects cannot be expected for the near future.

Besides these two factors, which tend to a more favourable development in NOPEC exports, some other qualifications may be made which rather point to an overstatement in the figures presented above. Additional exports will probably induce additional imports. An expansion in export production will need increased purchases of inputs, which at least partly have to be supplied by world markets. Furthermore, an enlarged export production will contribute to a general rise in income levels in NOPEC countries, thereby strengthening the demand for imported goods of all kinds. To the extent that this will not be counteracted by tightening protectionist measures—which, however, may severely impede the expansion in exports by adversely affecting the country's international competitiveness—the balance of payments effects of an improved export performance will be partly offset by rising imports.

Moreover, it has to be recalled that figures calculated above are rather sensitive to changes in OECD growth. If the scenario based on projections presented by the OECD and other international organisations is only slightly modified, this will have a noticeable impact. Taking, for example, a more sceptical view—that is, assuming that OECD growth will somewhat slacken down again to 2.5 per cent in 1985 and 1986 (Ahnefeld *et al.*, 1984, p. 16)—the amount of additional exports will be reduced to less than $21 billion (1985) and $27 billion (1986). It may be concluded, therefore, that an improvement in OECD growth may considerably help the NOPECs in easing their problems of servicing foreign debt. In order to be effective, however, the recovery in economic growth in the industrialised world must be rather strong. In addition, it has to emerge without further delay and must prevail for quite a long period. In other words, a lot of uncertainties still exist, so NOPECs should not exclusively place their confidence in better external economic conditions.

The same applies to other external factors which formerly added to NOPECs' debt difficulties and which may develop favourably in the coming years. Relief may be provided by a reduction in extraordinarily high international interest rates. A decrease of 1 percentage point in *average* interest rates paid by NOPECs would save them about $5.8 billion in foreign exchange in 1984.[3] This calculation is rather hypothetical, however. The share of floating-interest debt in total debt is still below 50 per cent (OECD, 1984, p. 36); that is, interest payments for less than half of total debt would be directly reduced by a change in interest rates prevailing in *international capital markets*. Assuming a reduction of 1 percentage point, the balance of payments effect dwindles to roughly $2.5 billion. Further accounting for some restructuring in fixed-interest debt at lower interest rates, the annual relief in debt servicing may be in the range of $3 billion to $3.5 billion. This amounts to less than 4 per cent of current-account deficits experienced in the early eighties.

In order to be of similar importance as the expansion in real exports (calculated at constant OECD-demand elasticities) the cost of foreign loans raised in international capital markets will have to decrease by about 5 percentage points. A drastic change in loan conditions cannot be expected, however. Although the US administration may succeed in constraining government budget-deficits to some extent, deficits will probably remain huge in the next few years, thereby keeping upward pressure on interest rates (Clausen, 1984, p.4). Moreover, in periods of expansion, interest rates typically rise rather than decrease (Meltzer, 1983, p.5). The most important Western central banks have announced that they will further cut the expansion in money supply in 1984. Restrictive monetary policies will probably be maintained till the peak in economic recovery has been reached (Ahnefeld *et al*., 1984, p.14). It is therefore hardly surprising that in an OECD forecast for 1984, average interest costs on developing countries' foreign debt (short-term loans excluded) are projected to rise slightly from 8.7 to 9 per cent (OECD, 1984, p.11). A significant relief in debt servicing through a more favourable development in international interest rates cannot be expected for the following years either.

Turning to the development in petroleum prices as a further external factor which may have a considerable impact on the NOPECs' balance of payments position, an even more grim picture emerges. It is rather tempting to make the following calculation: assuming another oil price reduction of $4 per barrel[4] and multiplying this price differential with a constant volume of developing countries' gross imports of crude oil and petroleum products of 3 billion barrels per year,[5] the oil importing economies in the Third World may save $12 billion in import payments. This calculation is strongly misleading, however. Certainly, financial strains of net oil importers would be eased by declining petroleum prices. It is rather idle, however, to speculate about future oil-price developments, remembering the bulk of completely erroneous estimations of the past. Accordingly, it is not certain whether there will be any relief at all, not to speak of its probable degree. It is, furthermore, often disregarded that quite a few oil exporters belong to the group of most heavily indebted countries. Their balance of payments and debt situation would be adversely affected by declining oil prices. For a group of twenty-one major Third World borrowers analysed by Morgan Guaranty Trust (which is nearly identical with our sample of eighteen countries), the net effect of lower oil prices would even be detrimental. This reflects the fact that the unfavourable consequences would be heavily concentrated among the net oil exporters in the group, whereas the benefits for net oil importers would be more widely dispersed (Morgan Guaranty Trust, June 1983, p. 10). Similarly, Cline concludes that 'a collapse in oil prices would seriously worsen the debt problem' (Cline, 1983, p. 72), notwithstanding mitigating indirect effects of lower oil prices, which would tend to stimulate economic growth, especially in industrial countries, and which may constrain worldwide inflation and therefore reduce upward pressures on nominal interest rates.

The results arrived at by Cline and Morgan Guaranty Trust are part of more general simulation models which, analytically, are far more pretentious than the rather crude estimates presented above (Cline, 1983, pp. 44–73; Morgan Guaranty Trust, February 1983, pp. 1–14, and June 1983, pp. 1–15). Compared to scepticism about significant debt relief automatically arising from improved international economic conditions, they take a somewhat more optimistic view. Cline concludes that the Third World's debt problem can be managed under reasonable assumptions. The debt situation is expected to show considerable improvement in the period 1984–86.

Some caveats, however, seem to be in place with regard to the reliability of model results. The outcome of the different simulations varies a good deal with respect to both country-specific and global forecasts. Comparing country-specific projections of the debt/export ratio, for example, the following picture emerges. For countries like Argentina and Brazil, Morgan Guaranty Trust presents considerably more pessimistic estimates than Cline (for 1985, 302 and 333 per cent versus 215 and 224 per cent, respectively). On the other hand, the Morgan Guaranty Trust figure for Chile is substantially lower than Cline's estimate (187 versus 255 per cent). The remarkable differences in global forecasts are indicated by Table 45, which compares projections of

Table 45: Different Projections of Non-Oil Developing Countries' Current-Account Balance, 1984–86 (in billions of US$)

	Cline[a]	Morgan Guaranty Trust[a]	IMF
1984	−64.1	n.a.	n.a.
1985	−53.2	−34.7	n.a.
1986	−52.5	n.a.	−93.0

[a] Calculated by applying 1982 ratios of the respective sample to all NOPECs.

Sources: Cline, 1983; Morgan Guaranty Trust, June 1983; IMF, 1983.

NOPECs' aggregated deficits in their current-account balance in the mid-eighties. The IMF estimate results in a deficit which is nearly twice as high as the figure given by Cline. Morgan Guaranty Trust is still considerably more optimistic. The forecasts differ so widely that it even remains an open question whether deficits will shrink at all compared to 1983. While Cline's and Morgan Guaranty Trust's answers are in the affirmative, the IMF predicts a rise in 1983 deficits by 37 per cent within three years.

Moreover, the simulation results are very sensitive to relatively small changes in key assumptions about world economic conditions from those used in the base case (Morgan Guaranty Trust, June 1983, p. 9). The debt/export ratio for the group of major Third World borrowers, for example, would scarcely improve during the eighties if OECD growth is only 1 percentage point lower than in the

base case. Applying scenarios which offer somewhat more
disturbing though not completely unrealistic prospects
'today's debt problems would only worsen' (Morgan Guaranty Trust, February 1983, p. 8).

This is why model results confirm rather than contradict
the conclusion that it would be dangerous to exclusively rely
on an improvement in external economic conditions. Both
the timing and the degree of a possible recovery of the global
economy remain highly uncertain. Even under relatively
favourable conditions, considerable time will probably be
required to substantially ease NOPECs' debt problems. The
foreign indebtedness of developing countries is therefore
likely to remain a central issue throughout the remainder of
this decade. A search for longer-term solutions seems
urgently required.

NOTES

1. The regression run was as follows:
    $$LGDP = a + b \cdot T$$
    where: LGDP = aggregated GDP of OECD member countries at
    constant prices of 1980 in logarithmic form
    T   = time trend
    a, b   = regression coefficients, where 'a' denotes the con-
    stant term and 'b' the annual average growth rate
    in GDP.
2. The following equation was estimated:
    $$LEX = a + b \cdot LGDP$$
    where: LEX   = exports of NOPECs to developed economies at
    constant prices of 1980 in logarithmic form
    a, b   = regression coefficients, where 'b' denotes the
    income elasticity of OECD member countries'
    imports from NOPECs.
3. The assumed change in interest rates is multiplied with NOPECs'
    total nominal (short-term and long-term) debt, net of reserves,
    outstanding at the end of 1983 (see Table 2, p. 8). International
    reserves have been deducted, since reserves are interest bearing,
    too, though the yield they provide for NOPECs will probably be
    somewhat lower than interest rates on the debit side.
4. This reduction would be comparable to the one experienced in
    1983. Calculating weighted average prices for crude petroleum
    exports of Saudi Arabia, Libya and Venezuela, the price per barrel

declined from $33.6 in 1982 to $29.4.
5.   The figure of 3 billion barrels per year is an average for 1980 and
       1981. More recent data were not available.

12   Reorganising International Debt: Longer-Term Proposals

Although the developing countries' indebtedness has only recently become an issue of public debate, the question of how to ease the Third World's debt burden has been discussed for almost two decades in various forums. In the late sixties the Pearson Commission (Pearson *et al.*, 1969, pp. 153–67) advocated debt relief as a legitimate form of development aid. The subject remained on the agenda in almost every round of North–South negotiations. The first aim of this chapter is to consider whether these former proposals can be fruitfully applied in the context of present debt difficulties. Second, the most important approaches which have recently been proposed as longer-term solutions of developing countries' debt problems will be critically reviewed.

In the field of North–South negotiations it has traditionally been the United Nations Conference on Trade and Development (UNCTAD) which has acted as an agent of developing countries' interests. On the list of measures that, in UNCTAD's view, should be implemented in order to improve the Third World's economic situation, demands for debt relief figured quite prominently. The Programme of Action of 1976 (UNCTAD, pp. 22–30) recommended that the least developed countries have their *official* debt cancelled. Furthermore, other Third World countries most seriously affected by an adverse international economic environment were to receive the same treatment, or at least have their service payments on official debt waived until they cease to be classified in this UN category. As regards *commercial* debt, UNCTAD asked for a long-term consolidation: debt-service payments were to be rescheduled over a period of at least twenty-five years. A new multilateral financial institution was to be established that would be designed to fund the Third World's short-term debt upon request. It was also proposed that a conference including the major developed creditor and affected debtor countries be convened, where a general framework of principles and guidelines on the renegotiation of official and commercial debt would be determined (for further details, see UNCTAD, 1977).

In addition to granting relief for old debt, the developed countries were asked to increase and improve the new funding of the Third World's capital needs. Official development assistance (ODA) was to be increased so as to achieve the 0.7 per cent (of the donor's GDP) target as soon as possible. The grant element of ODA was to be raised. To collect the required revenues, the introduction of a development tax in donor countries was proposed. In order to enlarge the ability of multilateral development finance institutions to lend to the Third World, developed countries were requested to increase their contributions to these institutions. The existing IMF policies were especially criticised. In UNCTAD's view the IMF should provide longer-term assistance at low interest rates and free of policy conditions in order to compensate for deteriorating international economic conditions. For example, the IMF's compensatory financing facility was to be substantially expanded. As regards commercial capital flows, capital exporting economies were to take measures to enhance the access of developing countries to their money and capital markets. Third World borrowers should be granted preferential treatment with respect to administrative requirements, statutory provisions and capital export controls. Financial obligations of developing countries should be officially guaranteed, either by individual governments or through multilateral facilities.

Notwithstanding that the UNCTAD's programme for debt relief included measures for dealing with commercial debt, it largely concentrated on official debt. Its implementation would therefore mainly help developing country groups that heavily depend on official assistance rather than those borrowers which nowadays stand as the main problem cases. It may be argued that the latter group could also benefit by using ODA as a substitute for commercial credits. However, the amount of available ODA funds would hardly suffice to substantially alleviate the debt burden of the largest debtor countries. Moreover, this would merely shift the financial strains to the traditional recipients of ODA, which would probably suffer a decline in commitments.

The UNCTAD programme has some further shortcomings. Debt-relief measures, as well as other proposals to ensure new financing, pose major moral hazard problems. The cancellation of old debt rewards mismanagement and the waste of foreign capital. On the other hand, recipients of ODA which had formerly strived for a punctual debt servicing would be punished retrospectively. This strategy would thus encourage those countries to abandon their sound debt management policies in order to benefit from retrospective debt cancellation in the future. The drawbacks arising from concessional IMF lending, for example, have already been discussed in Chapter 10. Problems of moral hazard would further deteriorate if UNCTAD's request to soften IMF conditionality is met.

Probably, UNCTAD's consideration of commercial debt in the Programme of Action was at least partly attributable to its attempt to ensure overall support for debt-relief measures in the Third World (Nunnenkamp, 1982b, p. 75; Boeck, 1977). More advanced developing countries, however, remained rather sceptical about global debt cancellation. They feared that the credit-worthiness of *all* developing countries would be negatively affected. Especially the Latin American borrowers were concerned that their standing in international capital markets would deteriorate. Lacking Third World solidarity and confronted with strong opposition from creditor countries, it was not surprising then that hardly any progress was achieved in the on-going North–South negotiations on debt problems.

In 1980 UNCTAD's proposals received strong support from the first 'Report of the Independent Commission on International Development Issues', under the chairmanship of Willy Brandt (Brandt *et al.*, 1980, pp. 267–92). Large parts of the Commission's recommendations concerning development finance consisted of a recapitulation of UNCTAD's demands. The threat of a grave financial crisis and doubts as to whether international debt could be adequately managed led the Commission to the conclusion that a large-scale transfer of resources to developing countries was urgently needed. It was recommended that the flow of ODA be significantly enlarged, for example, by introducing automatic revenue transfers through levies on international trade, arms production or sea-bed mineral mining. A further international financial institution—a World Development Fund—was to be created in order to satisfy unmet financial needs, especially in programme lending. The borrowing capacity of existing institutions was to be substantially increased. A reduction in the gold reserves of the IMF was also called for. The profits accruing from these gold sales would be used to subsidise interest rates on loans to the Third World. Furthermore, the Commission pleaded for an expansion of world liquidity via SDR creation. The distribution of SDRs would be linked to developing countries' financial needs.

The commercial banking system was urged to continue lending to the Third World. Official institutions were to provide concessional funds to be used for subsidising market rates of interest so that poorer countries could also take advantage of commercial loans. International institutions should guarantee the developing countries' liabilities and intensify co-financing in order to support commercial lending to these countries.

The Commission's recommendations can be criticised largely for the same reasons as the UNCTAD programme. An artificially reduced market-rate of interest for a specific group of borrowers is likely to result in a severe misallocation of capital. A significant expansion of international liquidity will probably result in additional inflationary pressures (i.e. the costs of adjustment will at least partly be socialised). By taxing international trade, the international division of labour according to the different producers' comparative advantages would be further distorted; this is likely to impede rather than alleviate the Third World's adjustment to changed international economic conditions, since the success of adjustment critically depends on increased export sales.

The Independent Commission also called for a joint effort to overcome the deadlock in North–South negotiations. For this purpose a summit meeting of political leaders from both industrialised and developing countries was proposed. This summit took place in Cancun, Mexico, in October 1981. But although the Third World's economic difficulties had further deteriorated in the meantime, hardly any progress was achieved in Cancun. This is particularly true with respect to the debt issue which, to the disappointment of the Independent Commission's chairman, received only scant attention (Brandt, 1981).

Not least of all, 'the acute dangers to the world's financial system' (Brandt *et al.*, 1983, p. 11) inspired the former members of the Independent Commission to present an updated version of their original programme. The recommendations have largely remained the same however. Strong official engagement by both national and multilateral institutions was regarded as indispensable.[1] The full implementation of waiving the service on official debt of the least developed countries was called for. Long-term borrowing was to be encouraged through officially sponsored issues of bonds. The resources for subsidising loans were to be further increased. The reluctance of smaller banks that were nervous about continuing lending under prevailing circumstances was to be overcome by official co-financing and guarantees. As an immediate response to acute debt problems, official bridging finance was to be extended. For this purpose creditor governments were asked to encourage their central banks to provide additional short-term deposits to the Bank for International Settlements. Furthermore, a rediscounting of some part of the developing countries' private bank debt was considered (Brandt *et al.*, 1983, pp. 93–4). An official agency would purchase banks' claims on developing countries at a discount (thereby assuming the banks' risk) and then renegotiate foreign debts at stretched-out maturities and reduced interest rates.

The Commission was confident that a realisation of these measures would help stabilise international capital markets and stimulate new commercial lending to the Third World. A strong official involvement may indeed ease financial strains in the short run. But the underlying causes of debt problems were hardly tackled by the Commission; especially domestic policy mistakes in the borrowing countries were largely neglected. This is why an implementation of the Commission's recommendations would not improve the credit-worthiness of highly indebted borrowers in the longer run, which alone would restore confidence on the side of commercial banks and revitalise private lending.

The moral hazard problem inherent in most of the proposals advanced by the Commission was only shortly addressed with respect to central banks' rescue operations (Brandt *et al.*, 1983, pp. 54–5). The probable long-term drawbacks of moral hazard—in this case, of the banks' possible reliance on the prospect of official rescue in their assessment of risks—were discounted. It was argued that moral hazard could be restrained by pressing commercial banks to continue lending; that is, by refusing a *major* substitution of public funds for the banks' lending. The remaining risks of moral hazard were obviously regarded as justified and inevitable in order to achieve the principal aim of preventing a worldwide financial collapse. This view will be challenged later on (see also Ch. 13).

In the programmes launched by the Independent Commission and UNCTAD, debt questions constituted only one issue, though a central one. Besides these rather comprehensive approaches as to how the Third World's economic difficulties could be overcome, the acute debt problems have provoked quite a few more specific studies.[2] The majority of these proposals, in common with the Independent Commission's and UNCTAD's recommendations, consider official intervention a necessity. According to this school of thought, part of the credit risk has to be assumed by the public. Differences remain, however, with respect to the way of sharing the burden among public and private parties involved (Bogdanowicz-Bindert, 1983, pp. 835–7):

1. Rohatyn proposes a scheme whereby banks' claims on developing countries would be converted into long-term, low-interest bonds issued by an existing or newly

created multilateral agency (Rohatyn, 1983). This entity would in turn offer debt relief to Third World borrowers by extending long-term funds at concessional interest rates. Rohatyn additionally envisages the need for creditor governments to be prepared to provide commercial banks with capital in order to solve liquidity problems. That would mean that the taxpayer has to bear part of the adjustment burden.

2. Similarly, Kenen proposes the purchase of banks' claims by a newly created International Debt Discount Corporation at a 10 per cent discount. This agency would then offer developing countries extended maturities and would use half of the discount for debt relief (Kenen, 1983).

3. Weinert suggests that the World Bank accepts up to 80 per cent of banks' claims on developing countries in exchange for long-term bonds (Weinert, 1983). Interest rates on bonds would be below market levels, the difference representing the burden to be absorbed by commercial banks. Interest rates would be tied to the borrowers' ability to pay, as indicated by a formula including export volumes and terms-of-trade. If a borrower proves unable to pay a minimum interest rate to the banks, the World Bank would have to pay the necessary difference; that is, the public might well share the cost of conversion.

4. According to a plan by Mackworth-Young, developing countries would fund balance of payments deficits by issuing bonds that carry an international guarantee. Assets already accrued from balance of payments lending would be put into an international secondary market in converted and officially guaranteed bank loans. The dominant concern is not debt relief but the banks' liquidity position. It is frankly admitted by Mackworth-Young that his scheme entails the socialisation of losses: 'The LDC bonds need to be guaranteed, so that if there is a default the whole developed world bears the weight, and not just the banks' (quoted in Grant, 1983, p. 58).

5. Leslie wants to improve the banks' liquidity position by

relieving them of the need to fund problem assets, without officially bailing out commercial creditors (Leslie, 1983). The purchase of problem loans by Western central banks at a discount is made conditional on the commercial banks' willingness to extend new loans—for example, export credits—in order to support domestic economic recovery. Moreover, credit risks would remain with the commercial banks since, if the borrowers were unable to pay, the bad loans would revert to the banks' accounts.

6. In a scheme proposed by Bailey, Luft and Robinson, the existing amortisation schedules would be replaced by newly created Exchange Participation Notes (Bailey, Luft, Robinson, 1983). These notes, issued by central banks of debtor countries to their creditors, would entitle commercial banks a certain share of the borrowing country's foreign exchange earnings. In other words, debt servicing is tied to the debtors' ability to repay.

7. Official intervention on the lenders' side is also avoided if both lending banks and borrowing countries would agree to convert the banks' loan claims into equity shares; for example, in state-owned enterprises (Krahnen, 1983; Meltzer, 1983). The banks would probably have to forego current income but would gain influence on the enterprises' policies and participate in profits later on.

8. A similar capital plan has been presented by the World Bank, though with official intermediation (*The Economist*, 24 March 1984). Shares of investment trusts for individual developing countries would be issued to participating commercial banks in exchange for their loans. The trust would then swap the foreign-currency loans into local-currency stakes in the borrowers' equity. The foreign exchange risk previously borne by the borrowers is taken over by the trust. The World Bank might also agree to assist the implementation of the scheme by providing some financial backing.

Although this list of proposals is far from complete, some typical features clearly emerge. Apart from rather specific shortcomings of individual schemes a more general criticism may be raised.[3] The approaches are primarily concerned with *old* debt, while *new* bank lending to the Third World is usually assumed to continue on a normal commercial basis. However, it is likely that an implementation of some of these schemes would severely affect new lending (Cline, 1983, pp. 117–18; Westphalen, 1984, p. 76; de Vries, 1983b, pp. 4–5).[4] After having escaped the lenders' trap via official bail-outs, the banks would probably refuse to participate in 'involuntary' lending in the future. This is to be expected all the more so as the plans presented above do not include any measures to restore the borrowers' credit-worthiness in the longer run, which alone would on economic grounds justify continued lending.

On the other hand, it has to be recalled that official interference in the burden sharing among creditors and borrowers and a socialisation of losses is likely to give rise to severe problems of moral hazard. If the access of developing countries to schemes providing for debt relief is conditional on being classified as a problem borrower, this would strongly encourage them to declare default. Debtors striving for economic adjustment in order to prevent or reduce financial strains would in effect be punished; hence, fewer would attempt to do so. Bailing out commercial banks would mean creating conditions where lenders can rely on official rescue and, therefore, discount risks in their lending decisions (Weintraub, 1983b, p. 7). Where moral hazard is ruled out, or at least largely restrained (for example, in schemes proposed by Meltzer, Krahnen, Leslie and by Bailey, Luft and Robinson), it is unlikely that commercial banks would participate in the schemes to a considerable extent. Lacking reasonable prospects of an improving credit-worthiness of borrowers in the longer run, there is hardly anything to gain for banks.

To ensure a continuous flow of funds to the Third World, it has been proposed that new bank lending should be officially guaranteed (Grant, 1983, p.61). However, as this would also shift risks from commercial banks to the public, the same criticism applies as to other forms of bail-outs.

As early as 1979, another way to encourage new lending

was advocated by Grubel. An International Deposit Insurance Corporation would insure deposits around the world (Grubel, 1979). The idea of insurance has been taken up recently. Wallich's scheme would cover credit-portfolios of banks rather than individual credits (Wallich, 1984). Besides reducing developing countries' difficulties in attracting further capital, this scheme is meant to serve as a safety net for commercial banks to prevent their collapse (and possible chain reactions) in case of major defaults of borrowers. Mainly, banks would help themselves; that is, they would have to fund the insurance scheme. In addition, financial contributions by both national and international official institutions are welcomed initially. But official assistance would then have to be paid back later in order to prevent misallocations of capital arising from a permanent subsidisation of international banking.

Undoubtedly, the possibility of shifting a part of the burden arising from non-performing loans to the taxpayer can be reduced by phasing out official assistance. But even if the insurance scheme entails no official participation at all, moral hazard is still likely to pose a problem. In order to rule out a run of bank creditors on their banks, a deposit insurance, for example, has to be comprehensive and complete. If coverage is not offered to large creditors (as in the United States' national deposit insurance system) or if deposits are not fully covered (so that all creditors of failed banks would suffer some loss) creditors are still likely to react with panic. On the other hand, 'insurance that is both comprehensive and complete presents enormous moral hazard. An insolvent bank ... can play go-for-broke indefinitely with what is essentially the insuring agency's funds' (Guttentag, Herring, 1983, p. 23).

Arguing that neither borrowers nor lenders 'should have to be bribed to pursue their own best interests' (Sjaastad, 1983, p. 319), another school of thought strongly opposes any official interference in the burden sharing among borrowers and lenders. Widespread contagion effects triggered by borrowers' defaults and possible bank collapses, in this view, can be prevented by formulating the lender-of-last-resort function of Western central banks in a way that rules out moral hazard (Ch. 13). It is because of the first-mentioned conviction that the threat of a debtors' cartel of developing countries, unilaterally refusing to service debt in a concerted action if significant debt relief is not officially granted, is largely discounted. Borrowers pursuing their own best interests are expected to reject such proposals, even after their credit standing has considerably deteriorated in the past. This is because countries participating in the formation of a debtors' cartel would probably be cut off from international capital markets for a long time. Actually, attempts to organise a united front and calls for joint action (almost exclusively to be heard from Latin America) have so far been restricted: cooperation among borrowers is aimed at pressing for more lenient repayment terms rather than the formation of a cartel that refuses to repay foreign debt.

Furthermore, all forms of bail-outs of debtor nations or creditor banks are criticised because of their high social costs (Brunner *et al.*, 1983). The commercial banks should decide on economic grounds alone whether to extend further loans or not, and not continue lending because the chances for a bail-out may improve in the meanwhile. 'The provision of additional loans without discrimination between permanent and transitory problems of debtors fosters incentives among debtor nations to continue policies that contribute to the current problem' (Brunner *et al.*, 1983, p. 162). Borrowers merely faced with *transitory* adjustment difficulties but offering bright economic prospects in the longer run should have no major problems in obtaining additional loans. It is most unlikely that commercial banks would miss profit opportunities inherent in lending to these countries. A *permanent* inability to repay, however, cannot be solved by additional loans. Whenever borrowers show little prospect of pursuing economic policies which are conducive to restoring their credit-worthiness, the problem of permanent default should be recognised at once in order to contain losses. Losses that have already been incurred by the banks should be borne by their management and shareholders.

This seems indeed to be the only way to ensure a productive use of capital. Long-term economic costs in terms of misallocations arising from moral hazard on the borrowers' or on the lenders' side are avoided. Both parties involved are provided with economically sound incentives. Borrowers can only succeed in raising additional funds when formulating domestic policies that seem well suited to improving the manageability of foreign debt. Lenders must carefully assess the risks involved in extending loans to different borrowers. Only in this way are existing problems likely to be overcome in the longer run and their recurrence prevented.

NOTES

1. The UNCTAD, too, largely insisted on its traditional approach (*see* UNCTAD, 1983, pp. 8–10). Most of the proposals of a two-year financial programme launched by the UNCTAD secretariat were also to be found in Brandt *et al.*, 1983. In view of the acute debt problems in the Third World, major emphasis was given to rather short-term emergency measures. Longer-term demands for a structural reform of the international monetary and financial system receded somewhat into the background compared with pre-crisis times.

2. An overview on the most well-known proposals is given in Bogdanowicz-Bindert, 1983, pp. 828–38; Cline, 1983, pp. 114–19; Grant, 1983, pp. 53–61; Nölling, 1983, pp. 86–94; Sandler, 1983, pp. 73–7.

3. To state just one example, the schemes launched by Weinert and by Bailey, Luft and Robinson may well weaken the borrowing countries' incentives to expand their world-market sales, since this would increase debt-service obligations.

4. The banks' willingness to continue lending would probably also be weakened if a limit ('cap') is imposed on interest rates charged by commercial banks to Third World borrowers. In the United States this idea has recently been advocated by the president of the Federal Reserve Bank of New York, Solomon, the Chairman of the Federal Reserve Board, Volcker, and the then Chairman of the Council of Economic Advisers, Feldstein (*The Financial Times*, 11 May 1984; *International Herald Tribune*, 14 May 1984). Moreover, interest rates below market standards would give rise to further misallocation of capital in the borrowing countries.

13 Elements of a Longer-term Solution of International Debt Problems: A Summary

The major aim of this book is to contribute to a lasting solution of developing countries' debt problems. Much has already been said in the preceding chapters, though frequently in a rather indirect way by evaluating concepts which, for various reasons, appear more or less inadequate for the task of eliminating the debt difficulties in the longer run. In what follows I will summarise the main findings of this study and the most important elements which need to be included in a longer-term strategy.

From the statistical analysis in the first part of this book it is clear that even within the sample of most important Third World borrowers, sharp differences prevail as to the degree of international indebtedness of individual developing countries and their debt-service burden. Moreover, not all the highly indebted borrowers experienced problems in raising and transferring their debt-service obligations; other countries faced repayment difficulties, although debt indicators pointed to a comparatively favourable debt position.

These differences are particularly remarkable as they cannot be attributed primarily to different degrees of impact on the balance of payments resulting from external shocks. The result that the group of countries suffering most from unfavourable world-market conditions is not identical with the set of borrowers with debt problems largely conflicts with conventional wisdom. The analysis of economic policies pursued by the debtor countries indicates that external disturbances could be mitigated by domestic adjustment measures. Especially those borrowers who failed to implement appropriate economic policy conditions ran into debt difficulties. At least for some of them, the debt situation seems to have deteriorated further, since the

Western creditor banks have not had sufficient incentives to abide by economically sound lending practices. The risk of loans granted to developing countries probably was discounted by commercial banks that felt safe against losses because the bulk of credits was raised by governments or was at least officially guaranteed. The banks could furthermore count on official rescue in their home countries since, according to a widespread view, they would have to be bailed out in case of major financial strains in order to prevent contagion effects.

Certainly some banks which strongly engaged in lending to the Third World are threatened by borrowers' defaults. Without official bail-outs, these may even force such banks to close down. Quite a few of the Third World's big borrowers continue to have considerable repayment difficulties, and their liabilities amount to a large portion of the banks' capital, especially in the case of US banks. It has also to be admitted that bank failures may trigger far-reaching chain reactions in the event of misconceived economic policy reactions in the industrialised world. The comparison of the economic environment prevailing in the twenties and thirties on the one hand and in the early eighties on the other revealed some similarities. If the mistrust of the banks' depositors is not restricted to certain banks perceived to be insolvent, and instead, depositors fear that they will lose their deposits, irrespective of where they are placed, a general run on banks may set in. Faced by an overall liquidity drain, banks would have to cut down loan provisions substantially. The financial crisis would then quickly impinge on the real economy and result in a severe contraction of production, employment and international trade on a worldwide scale.

It is undoubtedly the governments' responsibility to battle against another Great Depression. The 'public good' of preventing panic reactions of banks' depositors has to be officially provided. This should not be too difficult, however. Monetary authorities in the creditor countries have instruments at their disposal to counteract a liquidity crisis and probable contagion effects without socialising the banks' private losses. Central banks have to announce in advance that they will offset an increase in liquidity preference by the public by maintaining the expansion of money supply as scheduled. This would assure the commercial banks' depositors that monetary policies will not repeat the serious mistakes of the late twenties and early thirties when the money supply decreased drastically. If it is guaranteed that the collapse of a few insolvent banks will not result in an overall shortage in liquidity, public panic reactions would become less likely.

At present some confusion prevails in the mind of the general public about the crucial distinction between an official bail-out of insolvent banks and the central banks executing their lender-of-last-resort function (Brunner *et al.*, 1983, p. 165; Meltzer, 1983, p. 8). Public authorities should not provide a safety-net for insolvent commercial banks, their management and their shareholders, by transferring private losses of wealth to the taxpayers. This would be detrimental to a longer-term solution of debt problems as it gives rise to moral hazard. Commercial banks may then discount risks and continue lending to Third World borrowers, irrespective of whether the debtors offer reasonable prospects of improved economic conditions for servicing their foreign debt in the medium run or not. *All* banks have to bear their private losses, otherwise the allocation of capital will be distorted. If there is reason to believe that at least the large money-centre banks will be bailed out, depositors will quickly adjust and only deal with the top banks, thereby eroding the competitiveness of smaller banks (see, additionally, Robert Morris Associates, 1981, p. 5).

In contrast to official bail-outs of banks, the execution of a well-defined lender-of-last-resort function does not pose severe problems of moral hazard. An announcement that a widespread conversion of deposits into currency would be offset by the central banks' monetary policies would provide a safety-net for the public (that is not responsible for the banks' financial strains) rather than for insolvent commercial banks. Thus defined, the lender-of-last-resort function does not interfere with the commercial banks' risk assessment.

As regards actual policy, there is 'a calculated vagueness surrounding official arrangements to deal with an international banking crisis' (Guttentag, Herring, 1983, p. 18). In 1974 a communiqué was issued by central bankers from the major industrial countries meeting at the Bank for International Settlements. It says that the governors

had an exchange of views on the problem of the lender of last resort in the Euromarkets. They recognized that it would not be practical to lay down in advance detailed rules and procedures for the provision of temporary liquidity. But they were satisfied that means are available for that purpose and will be used if and when necessary.

That is, the central banks hesitate to publicly state what they are exactly able and prepared to do. This ambiguity may be justified if the lender-of-last-resort function were to generate moral hazard problems. However, if the central banks' role is appropriately defined, there is no need for vagueness. Moreover, the remaining uncertainties undermine depositors' confidence in the stability of the financial system and increase the probability of a general run on the banks. The communiqué may even be interpreted by depositors as indicating that at least the large banks will be officially bailed out. Accordingly, deposits will be placed in banks assumed to have been granted preferential treatment, which will distort interbank competition. This is why central banks should not only be prepared to perform their lender-of-last-resort function in a way that rules out moral hazard; they should also make explicit what they will and what they will not do.

A well-defined lender-of-last-resort function reduces the need of regulatory control and surveillance over the international operations of commercial banks (for details on the practice of bank supervision, see Dale, 1982). Only a lender-of-last-resort that induces moral hazard 'must have direct regulatory control over the institutions to which it is willing to provide assistance in order to limit the social costs of its actions (Guttentag, Herring, 1983, p. 13).

Finally, no existing or new *international* organisation is needed to perform an effective lender-of-last-resort function, as it is sometimes argued by reference to the substantially enlarged international banking activities. *National* central banks can cope with this even without taking 'a cosmopolitan view of their responsibilities' (Guttentag, Herring, 1983, p. 15). It is not only in the international but also in the national interest to offset an increased liquidity preference of banks' depositors via monetary policies. The 'Great Depression did not arise because national monetary authorities ignored their responsibility for the rest of the world, but because they acted against their own country's interest' (Vaubel, 1984, p. 13).

Against this background, the role of the International Monetary Fund in the restructuring of developing countries' debt should be defined as follows. A clear distinction has to be drawn between its function of devising economic policies, deemed as well suited to overcome debt problems in the longer run, and its own financial role.

With respect to the IMF's lending activities, doubts may be raised whether there is any need at all. Developing countries facing only transitory adjustment problems and offering favourable economic prospects in the longer run should have no major difficulties in raising loans from private sources. In the case of countries with permanent repayment problems, the IMF should not contribute to a further accumulation of losses by providing loans which have to be written off later. If this approach is regarded as too radical, IMF lending, as a minimum, should be subject to some reservations. Most importantly, further reschedulings should not be invited by subsidising IMF loans. Moreover, in order to contain additional inflationary pressures, the IMF's lending capacity should not be enlarged permanently when a squeeze in international liquidity is perceived to be only temporary; otherwise it is to be expected that the short-term easing of debt problems will result in even greater problems later.

The IMF may help to ensure further lending to the Third World by acting as a coordinating agent in the formation of bank consortia. However, commercial banks should not be officially pressed to maintain or expand lending, since the more compulsory such pressures are, the more banks may claim official bail-outs if loans must be declared as non-performing afterwards. It is certainly necessary that commercial banks continue to extend credits to the Third World wherever economically justifiable, since a sudden halt in lending is likely to aggravate debt problems; but each bank's decision should be a matter of their own responsibility and be based on economic grounds alone.

The formulation of economic adjustment programmes by the IMF is most important in this respect, since a borrower's readiness to comply with IMF's policy rules will significantly improve the chances for obtaining more credits from commercial banks. Undoubtedly, the typical design of policy programmes frequently implies considerable adjustment burdens for borrowing countries. But domestic policy failures which formerly contributed to the emergence of debt problems should be corrected without futher delay.

Broadly speaking, the way of re-orientation in domestic economic policies as prescribed by the IMF appears to be appropriate to restore the debtor nations' credit-worthiness in the longer run. Most importantly, governments' budget deficits should be reduced, inflation rates suppressed, overvalued exchange rates corrected, heavy short-term fluctuations in exchange rates stabilised and export production encouraged. Borrowers reshaping their economic policies in this way will have learnt one of the crucial lessons which emerged from the famous debate between Keynes and Ohlin on the German reparation problem fifty years ago (Keynes, 1929a; 1929b; Ohlin 1929a; 1929b). In order to ease their debt problems, borrowers have to improve their international competitiveness, a point which was made by Keynes. His advice given to the Germans is still valid for the present debtor nations in the Third World (Keynes, 1929a, pp. 3, 6–7):

the solution of the Transfer Problem must come about, in the main . . . by the diversion of German factors of production from other employments into the export industries . . . The easiest method would be to allow the exchange value of the German mark to fall by the amount required to give the necessary bounty to exports and then to resist any agitation to raise money-wages.

One important qualification has to be made, however, as regards the IMF's policy conditions and the most recent developments in the Third World's actual policies in the field of import policies. Required and actual reductions in a borrowing country's imports merely shift its debt problem to another borrower, especially where trade linkages between different borrowers are extensive. Accordingly, adjustment rules that make little sense when applied to many countries should be removed.

Major *internal* efforts of developing countries to strengthen their competitiveness in world markets are all the more important, as it remains highly uncertain as to whether, when and to what extent the Third World's financial strains will be eased by an improvement in *external* conditions (i.e. in the international economic environment). It would be extremely dangerous for debtor nations to exclusively rely on better external conditions. The scepticism about substantial improvements in the coming years notwithstanding, industrial countries should be pressed to play their part in easing the developing countries' critical debt situation without futher delay.

This is not to advocate an official bail-out of Third World borrowers. Most of the proposals aiming at debt relief (either by creditor governments taking over part of the expected losses of old debt or by officially subsidising new loans) should be rejected because of the moral hazard induced by a socialisation of losses. Other schemes that do not pose moral hazard problems may be implemented instead:

1. A conversion of debt into equity agreed upon by borrowers and creditors should be welcomed. In future, industrial countries should increase their direct investment in developing countries in order to reduce the need for new loans. However, this strategy is subject to the Third World's readiness to provide sufficient incentives for investment to take place.
2. A secondary market where bank loans are traded without governmental interference may help the banks to correctly assess the actual value of their portfolios. Losses which have to be borne by the lenders would be reflected far more exactly than by the present practice of writing down loans, which is rather arbitrary.

However, all these proposals have in common that they do

not include measures to restore the borrowers' credit-worthiness.

In order to contribute to a longer-term solution of developing countries' debt problems, the industrialised nations should tackle the causes rather than the mere symptoms of the present difficulties—as should the borrowers. Governments should be obliged to provide economic conditions that are well suited to foster economic growth. An increased import demand of industrial countries may significantly improve the manageability of developing countries' debt-service obligations. What has been called for in the case of borrowers should also be asked for in the case of creditor nations; that is, that they should bring their houses in order. As an important element of a growth-orientated strategy, the governments' shares in domestic absorption should be limited in order to avoid a crowding-out of a more productive private use of scarce resources. Furthermore, a reduction in governments' budget deficits, especially in the United States, may help to bring international interest rates down.

However, 'if markets are not kept open, and in many cases opened further, the worldwide recovery will be irrelevant to the debtor nations' (Feldstein, 1984, p. 7). In other words, just as the borrowers, so the creditor countries have to learn their lessons from the aforementioned Keynes/Ohlin debate. This time it is Ohlin who made the critical point (Ohlin, 1929a, p. 177):

If the policy of protection and of preference to home-made goods, which has been growing so much after the war, is intensified when German exports begin to grow, and is used consistently to prevent such exports, then the reparation payments may become virtually impossible.

To ease the developing countries' transfer problem, creditor countries have to adjust their own economies. This should include the phasing-out of subsidies granted to ailing industries and the liberalisation of all kinds of restrictive import practices. For example, developing countries should no longer be pressed to agree on 'voluntary' export restraints which at present severely impede a favourable world-market performance of Third World exporters, particularly in industries where they are most competitive. For many borrowing countries, a relaxation of trade restrictions is also most important in the field of agricultural products. The EEC, in particular, should be required to abolish its policy of 'orderly marketing' in agriculture.

It should by now be clear that it is no longer sufficient to continue muddling-through, which has so far dominated the short-term rescheduling approach. What is urgently needed, instead, is a strategy of policy re-orientation on both sides, the debtor and the creditor nations.

Bibliography

Abbott, G.C., *International Indebtedness and the Developing Countries* (Croom Helm: London 1979. Sharpe Inc., White Plains, N.Y. 1979)

Agarwal, J.P., Glismann, H.H., and Nunnenkamp, P., *Ölpreisschocks und wirtschaftliche Entwicklung. Anpassungsprobleme in der Dritten Welt* (J.C.B. Mohr: Tübingen 1983).

Ahnefeld, A., *et al.*, 'Am Rande der Krise', *Kiel Discussion Paper*, No. 89 (Kiel 1982)

——, 'Nachhaltiger Aufschwung oder Wellblechkonjunktur? Thesen zum 29. Kieler Konjunkturgespräch, *Kiel Discussion Paper*, No. 97 (Kiel 1984)

Aliber, R.Z., 'A Conceptual Approach to the Analysis of External Debt of the Developing Countries', *World Bank Staff Working Paper*, No. 421 (Washington 1980)

Anderson, T., 'The Year of the Rescheduling', *Euromoney*, August 1982, pp. 19–22

Arndt, H.W., *The Economic Lessons of the Nineteen Thirties* (Oxford University Press: London, New York, Toronto 1944)

Aspe Armella, P., Dornbusch, R., and Obstfeld, M., *Financial Policies and the World Capital Market: The Problem of Latin American Countries* (University of Chicago Press: Chicago, London 1983)

Avramovic, D., *Debt Servicing Capacity and Post-War Growth in International Indebtedness* (John Hopkins Press: Baltimore 1958)

——, *et al.*, *Economic Growth and External Debt* (Johns Hopkins Press: Baltimore 1964)

Bacha, E.L., and Díaz Alejandro, C.F., 'International Financial Intermediation: A Long and Tropical View', *Essays in International Finance*, No. 147 (Princeton University: Princeton 1982)

Bailey, N.A., Luft, R.D., and Robinson, R.H., 'Exchange

Participation Notes: An Approach to the International Financial Crisis' in *The International Financial Crisis: An Opportunity for Constructive Action*, ed. T. de Saint Phalle (Georgetown University Center for Strategic and International Studies: Washington 1983), pp. 27–36

Balassa, B., 1981a, 'The Newly-Industrializing Developing Countries after the Oil Crisis', *Weltwirtschaftliches Archiv*, 117 (1981), pp. 142–94

——, 1981b, 'Policy Responses to External Shocks in Selected Latin American Countries', *The Quarterly Review of Economics and Business*, 21 (1981), pp. 131–64

Bank for International Settlements (BIS), *Annual Report* (Basle, var. iss.)

——, *International Banking Developments* (Basle, var. iss.)

——, *The Maturity Structure of International Bank Lending* (Basle, var. iss.)

Beloff, N., 'Yugoslavia: IMF's Mission Impossible', *The Wall Street Journal*, 12 October 1983

Bernanke, B. S., 'Nonmonetary Effects of the Financial Crisis in the Propagation of the Great Depression', *American Economic Review*, 73 (1983), pp. 257–75

Blanchard, O. J., 'Debt and the Current Account Deficit in Brazil' in *Financial Policies and the World Capital Market: The Problem of Latin American Countries*, ed. P. Aspe Armella, R. Dornbusch, and M. Obstfeld (University of Chicago Press: Chicago, London 1983), pp. 187–97

Boeck, K., 'Finanzierungsprobleme im Rahmen des Nord-Süd-Dialogs' in *Europa und der Nord-Süd-Dialog*, ed. W. Wessels (Europa Union Verlag: Bonn 1977), pp. 51–64

Bogdanowicz-Bindert, C. A., 'Debt: Beyond the Quick Fix', *Third World Quarterly*, 5 (1983), pp. 828–38

Brandt, W., 'Progress by the Millimetre at Cancun', *The Economist*, 28 November 1981

——, et al., *North-South: A Programme for Survival* (Pan Books: London, Sydney 1980)

—— ——, *Common Crisis. North-South: Cooperation for World Recovery* (Pan Books: London, Sydney 1983)

Brau, E., Williams, R. C., et al., 'Recent Multilateral Debt Restructurings with Official and Bank Creditors', *IMF*

Occasional Paper, No. 25 (Washington 1983)

Brunner, K. (ed.), *The Great Depression Revisited* (Nijhoff: Boston, The Hague, London 1981)

———, *et al.*, 'International Debt, Insolvency and Illiquidity', *Journal of Economic Affairs*, 3 (1983), pp. 160–6

Buchanan, J. M., 'From Private Preferences to Public Philosophy: The Development of Public Choice' in *The Economics of Politics* (The Institute of Economic Affairs: London 1978), pp. 1–20

Bundesverband Deutscher Banken (ed.), *International Banking: Its New Dimensions* (Bank-Verlag: Köln 1981)

Clausen, A. W., 'Third World Debt and Global Recovery', *Aussenwirtschaft*, 38 (1983), pp. 249–61

———, *Priority Issues for 1984. Remarks as Prepared for Delivery before the European Management Forum* (unpublished manuscript, Washington 1984)

Cline, W. R., *International Debt and the Stability of the World Economy* (Institute for International Economics: Washington 1983. Distributed by MIT Press: London)

Crockett, A. D., 'Stabilization Policies in Developing Countries: Some Policy Considerations', *IMF Staff Papers*, 28 (1981), pp. 54–79

Dale, R., *Bank Supervision Around the World* (Group of Thirty: New York 1982)

Dennis, G. E. J., 'The Growth of International Bank Lending, 1972–1982. Concepts, Measurement and Causes', *Aussenwirtschaft*, 38 (1983), pp. 263–83

Deutsche Bundesbank, *Geschäftsbericht für das Jahr 1983* (Frankfurt 1984)

Dhonte, P., *Clockwork Debt* (Lexington Books: Lexington, Toronto 1979)

Diamond, D. W., and Dybvig, Ph. H., 'Bank Runs, Deposit Insurance, and Liquidity', *Journal of Political Economy*, 91 (1983), pp. 401–19

Díaz Alejandro, C. F., 'Stories of the 1930s for the 1980s' in *Financial Policies and the World Capital Market: The Problem of Latin American Countries*, ed. P. Aspe Armella, R. Dornbusch, and M. Obstfeld (University of Chicago Press: Chicago, London 1983), pp. 5–35

Eaton, J., and Gersovitz, M., 1981a, 'Debt with Potential

Repudiation: Theoretical and Empirical Analysis', *Review of Economic Studies*, 48 (1981), pp. 289–309

—— ——, 1981b, 'Poor-Country Borrowing in Private Financial Markets and the Repudiation Issue', *Princeton Studies in International Finance*, No. 47 (Princeton 1981)

Federal Reserve Board of Governors, *Country Exposure Lending Survey* (Washington, var. iss.)

Feldstein, M., *International Debt Policy: The Next Steps* (unpublished manuscript, Washington 1984)

Finch, D., 'Investment Service of Under-Developed Countries', *IMF Staff Papers*, 2 (1951), pp. 60–85

Fleming, A. E., 'Private Capital Flows to Developing Countries and Their Determination: Historical Perspectives, Recent Experience, and Future Prospects', *World Bank Staff Working Paper*, No. 484 (Washington 1981)

——, and Howson, S. K., 'Conditions in the Syndicated Medium-Term Euro-Credit Market', *Bank of England Quarterly Bulletin*, 20 (1980), pp. 311–18

Franko, L. G., 'Debt, Trade, and the Prospects for World Economic Growth' in *Developing Country Debt*, ed. L. G. Franko, and M. J. Seiber (Pergamon Press: New York 1979), pp. 284–98

——, and Seiber, M. J. (ed.), *Developing Country Debt* (Pergamon Press: New York 1979)

Friedman, M., and Schwartz, A. J., *The Great Contraction 1929–1933* (Princeton University Press: Princeton 1967)

Ganoe, Ch. S., 'Loans to LDCs: Five Myths' in *Developing Country Debt*, ed. L. G. Franko, and M. J. Seiber (Pergamon Press: New York 1979), pp. 81–90

Giersch, H., '8-Point Plan for Escape from Stagnation', *Journal of Economic Affairs*, 2 (1982), pp. 205–10

Glismann, H. H., and Nunnenkamp, P., 'Die Entwicklungsländer am Rande einer Verschuldungskrise. Überlegungen zu den Ursachen und Folgen am Beispiel Lateinamerikas', *Kiel Discussion Paper*, No. 91 (Kiel 1983)

——, and Rodemer, H., 'Der wirtschaftliche Niedergang in der Bundesrepublik Deutschland und in der Weimarer Republik', *Kiel Working Paper*, No. 154 (Kiel 1982)

—— ——, and Wolter, F., 'Long Waves in Economic Development. Causes and Empirical Evidence' in *Long*

Waves in the World Economy, ed. C. Freeman (Butterworths: London, Boston 1983), pp. 135–63

Gold, J., 'Financial Assistance by the International Monetary Fund: Law and Practice', *IMF Pamphlet Series*, No. 27 (Washington 1979)

Goodman, L. S., 'Bank Lending to Non-OPEC LDCs: Are Risks Diversifiable?', *Federal Reserve Bank of New York Quarterly Review*, 6 (1981), No. 2, pp. 10–20

Grant, Ch., 'Those Debt Proposals: Radical or Just Wrong?', *Euromoney*, July 1983, pp. 53–61

de Grauwe, P., and Fratianni, M., *The Political Economy of International Lending* (unpublished manuscript, 1983)

Greiff, P., and Martin, E. G., 'Venezuela May Seek Giant Bank Loan to Bring Order to Chaotic Debt Picture', *The Wall Street Journal*, 17 March 1981

Group of Thirty, *Risks in International Bank Lending* (Group of Thirty: New York 1982)

Grubel, H. G., 'A Proposal for the Establishment of an International Deposit Insurance Corporation', *Essays in International Finance*, No. 133 (Princeton University: Princeton 1979)

Guth, W., 'Trends in International Banking' in *International Banking: Its New Dimensions*, ed. Bundesverband Deutscher Banken (Bank-Verlag: Köln 1981), pp. 9–24

Guttentag, J., and Herring, R., 'The Lender-of-Last-Resort Function in an International Context', *Essays in International Finance*, No. 151 (Princeton University: Princeton 1983)

Haberler, G., *The World Economy, Money, and the Great Depression 1919–1939* (American Enterprise Institute for Public Policy Research: Washington 1976)

Hardy, Ch. S., *Rescheduling Developing-Country Debts, 1956–1981: Lessons and Recommendations* (Overseas Development Council: Washington 1982)

Hastings, N., 'Colombia Seeks Loan, in Test of Wariness in Euromarkets', *The Wall Street Journal*, 8 July 1983

Holthus, M., 'Lessons from the Debt Crisis', *Intereconomics*, 19 (1984), pp. 49–50

Hope, N. C., 'Developments in and Prospects for the External Debt of Developing Countries: 1970–80 and Beyond',

World Bank Staff Working Paper, No. 488 (Washington 1981)

Inoue, K., 'Determinants of Market Conditions in the Eurocurrency Market. Why a "Borrowers' Market"?', *BIS Working Paper*, No. 1 (Basle 1980)

Institutional Investor Magazine (New York, var. iss.)

International Monetary Fund (IMF), *Annual Report* (Washington, var. iss.)

——, *Annual Report on Exchange Arrangements and Exchange Restrictions* (Washington, var. iss.)

——, *International Financial Statistics* (Washington, var. iss.)

——, *International Financial Statistics. Supplement on Fund Accounts*, Supplement Series, No. 3 (Washington 1982)

——, *World Economic Outlook* (Washington 1983).

Johnson, G.G., 'Aspects of the International Banking Safety Net', *IMF Occasional Paper*, No. 17 (Washington 1983)

Johnston, R.B., 'Banks' International Lending Decisions and the Determination of Spreads on Syndicated Medium-Term Euro-Credits', *Bank of England Discussion Paper*, No. 12 (London 1980)

——, *The Economics of the Euro-Market: History, Theory and Policy* (Macmillan Press: London 1983)

Kenen, P., 'A Bailout Plan for the Banks', *The New York Times*, 6 March 1983

Keynes, J.M., 1929a, 'The German Transfer Problem', *The Economic Journal*, 39 (1929), pp. 1–7

——, 1929b, 'Mr. Keynes' Views on the Transfer Problem, III. A Reply by Mr. Keynes', *The Economic Journal*, 39 (1929), pp. 404–8

Khan, M.S., and Knight, M.D., 'Stabilization Programs in Developing Countries: A Formal Framework', *IMF Staff Papers*, 28 (1981), pp. 1–53

—— ——, 'Sources of Payments Problems in LDCs', *Finance and Development*, 20 (1983), No. 4, pp. 2–5

Kindleberger, Ch.P., *The World Depression 1929–1939* (Lane: London 1973)

——, *Manias, Panics, and Crashes. A History of Financial Crises* (Macmillan: London 1978)

Krahnen, H.J., 'Warum nicht Forderungen in Kapital

umwandeln?', *Frankfurter Allgemeine Zeitung*, 13 December 1983

Lee, J., 'Long-Run Debt Servicing Capacity of Asian Developing Countries: An Application of Critical Interest Rate Approach', *Asian Development Bank Economic Staff Paper*, No. 16 (Manila 1983)

Leslie, P., 'Techniques of Rescheduling: The Latest Lessons', *The Banker*, April 1983, pp. 23–30

Llewellyn, D.T., 'International Banking in the 1970s: An Overview' in *A Framework of International Banking*, ed. S.F. Frowen (Guildford Educational Press: Guildford 1979), pp. 25–54

Madden, J.T., Nadler, M., and Sauvain, H., *America's Experience as a Creditor Nation* (Prentice-Hall: New York 1937)

Mayer, H., 'The BIS Concept of the Eurocurrency Market', *Euromoney*, May 1976, pp. 60–6

Meltzer, A.H., *Notes on the Problem of International Debt* (unpublished manuscript, 1983)

Mendelsohn, M.S., *Commercial Banks and the Restructuring of Cross-Border Debt* (Group of Thirty: New York 1983)

Morgan Guaranty Trust, *World Financial Markets* (New York, var. iss.)

Navarrete, J.E., 'External Debt of Developing Countries at the Paris Conference: Positions, Proposals and Conclusions' in *LDC External Debt and the World Economy*, ed. M.S. Wionczek (El Colegio de México and Center for Economic and Social Studies of the Third World: Mexico City 1978), pp. 119–44

Niskanen, W.A., *Bureaucracy and Representative Government* (Aldine-Atherton: Chicago, New York 1971)

Noellert, W.A., 'The International Debt of Developing Countries and Global Economic Adjustment' in *Developing Country Debt*, ed. L.G. Franko, and M.J. Seiber (Pergamon Press: New York 1979), pp. 269–83

Nölling, W., 'Die Krise bändigen', *Wirtschaftswoche*, 14 October 1983, pp. 86–94

Nowzad, B., Williams, R.C.,*et al.*, 'External Indebtedness of Developing Countries', *IMF Occasional Paper*, No. 3 (Washington 1981)

Nunnenkamp, P., 'Negative Weltmarkteinflüsse und Anpassungsreaktionen in Brasilien und Südkorea', *Die Weltwirtschaft*, 1979, pp. 111–34

——, 1982a, 'The Impact of Rising Oil Prices on Economic Growth in Developing Countries in the Seventies', *Kyklos*, 35 (1982), pp. 633–47

——, 1982b, 'Der Nord-Süd-Dialog. Zwischenperiode vielfältiger Detailverhandlungen vor UNCTAD V' in *Die Internationale Politik 1977–1978*, ed. W. Wagner *et al.* (R. Oldenbourg: München, Wien 1982), pp. 67–79

——, 'Rising Oil Prices and Industrial Production in Some Developing Countries in the Seventies', *Asian Economies*, 47 (1983), pp. 26–40

O'Brien, R. R., 'Private Bank Lending to Developing Countries', *World Bank Staff Working Paper*, No. 482 (Washington 1981)

Ohlin, B., 1929a, 'The Reparation Problem: A Discussion, I. Transfer Difficulties, Real and Imagined', *The Economic Journal*, 39 (1929), pp. 172–8

——, 1929b, 'Mr. Keynes' Views on the Transfer Problem, II. A Rejoinder from Professor Ohlin', *The Economic Journal*, 39 (1929), pp. 400–4

Organisation for Economic Co-operation and Development (OECD), *Development Co-operation* (Paris, var. iss.)

——, *Financial Statistics* (Paris, var. iss.)

——, *Debt Problems of Developing Countries* (Paris 1974)

——, *External Debt of Developing Countries, 1982 Survey* (Paris 1982)

——, *External Debt of Developing Countries, 1983 Survey* (Paris 1984)

Palmer, J., *et al.*, 'The Debt-Bomb Threat', *Time*, 10 January 1983

Pearson, L. B., *et al.*, *Partners in Development. Report of the Commission on International Development* (Praeger Publishers: New York, Washington, London 1969)

Petersen, H. J., 'Debt Crises of Developing Countries: A Pragmatic Approach to an Early Warning System', *Konjunkturpolitik*, 23 (1977), pp. 94–110

Pöhl, K.-O., 'Central Banks and the New Dimensions in International Banking' in *International Banking: Its New*

Dimensions, ed. Bundesverband Deutscher Banken (Bank-Verlag: Köln 1981), pp. 25–38

Porzecanski, A. C., 'The International Financial Role of US Commercial Banks: Past and Future', *Journal of Banking and Finance*, 5 (1981), pp. 5–16

Prudential-Bache Securities, *Banking Industry Outlook*, 6 May 1983

Robert Morris Associates, *An Integrated Approach to Foreign Bank Analysis* (Philadelphia 1981)

Rohatyn, F., 'A Plan for Stretching Out Global Debt', *Business Week*, 28 February 1983

Rowley, Ch. K., 'Buying Out the Obstructors?' in *The Taming of Government* (The Institute of Economic Affairs: London 1979), pp. 107–18

Sachs, J., 'LDC Debt in the 1980s: Risk and Reforms' in *Crises in the Economic and Financial Structure*, ed. P. Wachtel (Lexington Books: Lexington, Toronto 1982), pp. 197–244

——, 'Theoretical Issues in International Borrowing', *National Bureau of Economic Research Working Paper*, No. 1189 (Cambridge 1983)

——, Cohen, D., 'LDC Borrowing with Default Risk', *National Bureau of Economic Research Working Paper*, No. 925 (Cambridge 1982)

Salomon Brothers, *US Multinational Banking Semi-Annual Statistics* (New York 1980)

Sandler, L., 'Is Discounting Sovereign Debt the Way Out?', *Institutional Investor Magazine*, July 1983, pp. 73–7

Sjaastad, L. A., 'International Debt Quagmire—to Whom Do We Owe It?', *The World Economy*, 6 (1983), pp. 305–24

Solomon, R., 'A Quantitative Perspective on the Debt of Developing Countries' in *Developing Country Debt*, ed. L. G. Franko, and M. J. Seiber (Pergamon Press: New York 1979), pp. 17–41

——, 'The Debt of Developing Countries: Another Look', *Brookings Papers on Economic Activity*, 1981, No. 2, pp. 593–606 (Washington 1982)

United Nations (UN), *Monthly Bulletin of Statistics* (New York, var. iss.)

——, *Yearbook of International Trade Statistics* (New York, var. iss.)

——, *Yearbook of World Energy Statistics* (New York, var. iss.)

United Nations Conference on Trade and Development (UNCTAD), *Manila Declaration and Programme of Action*, TD/195, 12 February 1976

——, *Selected Issues Relating to the Establishment of Common Norms in Future Debt Reorganizations*, TD/AC. 2/9, 31 October 1977

——, 1983a, *Handbook of International Trade and Development Statistics* (New York 1983)

——, 1983b, 'Key Reports for UNCTAD VI Propose New Policies and Measures in Fields of Commodities, Trade and Finance', *UNCTAD Bulletin*, No. 191, February/March 1983, pp. 1–10

Vaubel, R., 1983a, 'Coordination or Competition among National Macroeconomic Policies?' in *Reflections on a Troubled World Economy. Essays in Honour of Herbert Giersch*, ed. F. Machlup, G. Fels, and H. Müller-Groeling (Trade Policy Research Centre: London 1983), pp. 3–28

——, 1983b, 'The Moral Hazard of IMF Lending', *The World Economy*, 6 (1983), pp. 291–303

——, *International Debt, Bank Failures and the Money Supply: The Thirties and the Eighties* (unpublished manuscript, 1984)

de Vries, B. A., 1983a, *Composition and Direction of Manufactured Exports and the Financial Viability of Debtor Countries* (unpublished manuscript, 1983)

——, 1983b, *International Ramifications of the External Debt Situation* (unpublished manuscript, 1983)

Wallich, H. C., 'Central Banks as Regulators and Lenders of Last Resort in an International Context: A View from the United States' in *Key Issues in International Banking, The Federal Reserve Bank of Boston Conference Series*, No. 18 (Boston 1977), pp. 91–8

——, 'Insurance of Bank Lending to Developing Countries', *Group of Thirty Occasional Paper*, No. 15 (New York 1984)

Weinert, R. S., 'Banks and Bankruptcy', *Foreign Policy*,

No. 50, Spring 1983, pp. 138–49

Weintraub, R.E., 1983a, *International Debt: Crisis and Challenge* (George Mason University: Fairfax 1983)

——, 1983b, *International Lending by US Banks: Practices, Problems, and Policies* (George Mason University: Fairfax 1983)

Westphalen, J., 'Origin and Consequences of the Debt Crisis and Ways of Solving It', *Intereconomics*, 19 (1984), pp. 71–7

Williams, R.C., *et al.*, 'International Capital Markets. Developments and Prospects, 1982', *IMF Occasional Paper*, No. 14 (Washington 1982)

Williamson, J., *The Lending Policies of the International Monetary Fund* (Institute for International Economics: Washington 1982)

Wionczek, M.S., *et al.*, 'External Indebtedness of the Developing Countries' in *LDC External Debt and the World Economy*, ed. M.S. Wionczek (El Colegio de México and Center for Economic and Social Studies of the Third World: Mexico City 1978), pp. 9–118

World Bank, *Borrowing in International Capital Markets* (Washington, var. iss.)

——, *World Debt Tables* (Washington, var. iss.)

——, *World Development Report* (Washington, var. iss.)

——, *Prospects for Developing Countries, 1978–85* (Washington 1977)

Author Index

Subject Index